To Tom:
A fellow man
on the journey
so far.

[signature]

THE RIDE SO FAR

THE RIDE SO FAR

Tales from a Motorcycling Life

Lance Oliver

Whitehorse Press
Center Conway, New Hampshire

Illustrations and cover art by Craig Harrison. Author photos by Sarah Heidt.

We recognize that some words, model names and designations mentioned herein are the property of the trademark holder. We use them for identification purposes only.

Whitehorse Press books are also available at discounts in bulk quantity for sales and promotional use. For details about special sales or for a catalog of motorcycling books, videos, and gear write to the publisher:

Whitehorse Press
107 East Conway Road
Center Conway, New Hampshire 03813
Phone: 603-356-6556 or 800-531-1133
E-mail: CustomerService@WhitehorsePress.com
Internet: www.WhitehorsePress.com

ISBN-10 1-884313-88-4
ISBN-13 978-1-884313-88-2

5   4   3   2   1

Printed in United States

For Ivonne, who makes the ride home the most important part of every journey.

CONTENTS

PART 1
GREAT PLACES &
MEMORABLE RIDES

PART 2
RUMINATIONS
& MEDITATIONS

PREFACE

Odds are, if you've picked up this book, then you're just a little excessively interested in motorcycles, like me. You might say that I had no choice but to write it, because after spending such an inordinate share of my finite time on this earth thinking about, talking about, and writing about motorcycle stuff, I had to do *something* with all those words.

Anyone who's been riding for any amount of time has accumulated more than a few stories. Mine is not the most outstanding motorcycling life and career in history, I readily admit. I haven't ridden around the world, qualified for a World Superbike grid or expertly restored a priceless vintage bike that's currently on display in a major museum. These days, when it sometimes seems like darn near everyone has not only been to Alaska and back, but also has a blog about the trip and is selling a DVD of the journey, I have to admit I haven't made it to the Arctic Circle (frankly, it sounds a bit chilly for my tastes). But I have seen my share of memorable destinations and I've done a few oddball rides of the kind that are often even more fun in the retelling than they were in the moment.

So these are some of my motorcycling stories. They are divided into two sections. Part 1, Great Places & Memorable Rides, consists of my portraits in words of some of the more interesting destinations I've visited, from the peak of Mount Washington in New Hampshire to ancient ruins in Mexico, and some of the stranger rides I've undertaken, such as flogging a little Suzuki GN125 non-stop around Lake Erie in a charity fundraiser. Just about all of these destinations are places you could probably ride to yourself. Maybe you've already been to several of them. If so, I hope these stories bring back memories and maybe add an odd fact or observation you didn't pick up on when you passed by. Or maybe they'll inspire you to set off for destinations you haven't considered before. Part II, Ruminations & Meditations, contains my takes on the kinds of things we talk about when the kickstands are down, from memories of your first bike to speculation on motorcycling in the future.

I hope you enjoy these tales and that at some point they make you nod in recognition and say, "Yes, that's just the way it feels." I also hope they inspire you to get out and live some new motorcycle stories of your own. Meanwhile, please cut me some slack for not having made that Arctic Circle trip. That's why the book is called *The Ride So Far*. I'm not done yet.

INTRODUCTION

Here's possibly the one thing I've learned over my years of motorcycling experience that is least likely to come in handy. If you stop at a small country gas station where the resident mutt is a three-legged pit-bull mix that is enraged by the sound of a Harley-Davidson V-twin, don't be fooled by the speed at which he is approaching your leg. Out of the corner of your eye, the slow-moving dog may appear to be ambling your way in an unthreatening, even genial fashion. In fact, because he has three legs, he's charging as fast and furious as he can, and although his shortage of legs may impede his speed, his jaws and teeth still leave a mark. True story. I have the scar to prove it. One of those teeth got me right above the boot.

As you can see, this is not a book of useful advice. There are some great books out there by experts who can teach you how to ride better, and plenty of guidebooks that will tell you where to go, the best way to get there, which hotels to stay in, and what sights must not be missed. But while this book has to be classified more as entertainment than information, I'd like to think there's a little wisdom between the covers. On my personal ride so far, I've tried to benefit from lessons learned and I flatter myself to be a thinking rider's rider. I don't put up much of an argument now and then when someone suggests that I think too much. Sometimes I do get a little carried away with considering all the pros and cons and examining every possible angle when I should just choose a direction and roll on the throttle.

But that's partially because my approach to most things in life is to try to do as much as possible by conscious, informed choice and as little as possible by random chance, and that holds true for motorcycling. I do not ride motorcycles, write about motorcycles, and spend way too much of my time thinking about motorcycling because of happenstance. Unlike Miguel Duhamel or Willie G. Davidson, I am not the son of a motorcycle racer or the grandson of a guy whose name is on millions of gas tanks, so I was not influenced from the beginning by nature and nurture, by ancestral DNA and family environment, to ride these inherently unstable contraptions. On both personal and professional levels, it's a decision. It's something I want to do and often I have to find ways to make it happen, sometimes even when it would be easier not to or more lucrative to do something else. "*Cogito ergo sum*," said French philosopher René Descartes—though he actually said it first in French, not Latin. "I think, therefore I am," is the common English translation. Because he thinks, he can be certain he exists. My personal version of that old saying is entirely more pedestrian and far less ground-breaking: I think, therefore I ride. It's one of the things I can be certain of about myself, a part of my identity. But it's not just an emotional choice. I argue it's also a rational one.

We typically think of riding a motorcycle as an emotional decision. It's something we like. It's fun. It's adventurous. In the eyes of some, it makes us look cool (or so we hope). Or maybe we were the kid who saw the bright red motorcycle parked at the curb and instantly knew, with no warning but beyond any doubt, that someday we had to have one of our own. Most often, riding is about feelings, both the emotional responses our bikes evoke and the physical sensations we experience when we ride them.

But if that's all there were to it, I'd feel that something was missing. I want to ride because of both sides of my brain—and, I believe I do. Actually, I'm convinced that it makes good, rational sense for me to keep doing it for as long into life as my health permits. I ride far more often for transportation than just for fun, but motorcycling injects fun into my transportation, and thus into my daily life, and that helps stave off impending geezerdom.

In the days when I worked in an office and had a morning commute like normal people, I'd arrive by motorcycle, darting lightly through traffic and zipping ahead of lumbering trucks. I'd park in the special motorcycling parking area, and inevitably think: Why would I want to be just another droplet in an ocean of cars? Why would I trade my barracuda for a manatee? I'd arrive at the office more alert, more alive, than any of my co-workers in their convenient, conventional cars. What's that worth in dollars and good sense? How much does therapy cost?

I think, therefore I ride. And even though this is definitely no "how-to" book, and leans more toward armchair reading than desktop studying, I have indulged in the mental game of trying to choose the single best piece of riding advice I've ever been given. I think it comes down to one phrase: Look where you want to go. I know, that falls short of profound, eloquent or original. Deeper lessons could certainly be gleaned from a motorcycling life, but none more useful. Whether you're a wobbly newbie just trying to get through the cones in the Department of Motor Vehicles parking lot and earn your license, or a expert-level amateur racer who's a little too hot into turn seven on the last lap of the race, looking where you want to go is the one action most likely to spare you disappointment, heartache and broken fairings. Its power lies in how it brings together the way the human body works, on its own ("Keep your eye on the ball," in other sports) and the way the human body interacts with a machine.

It's also powerful advice because of how well it applies to life in general. Keep your eyes on your goals, keep your focus sharp, and you'll be less likely to end up some place you never wished to be, whether that's falling into a rut in life or into a ditch on your bike. And that, far more than hard-earned but useless wisdom about three-legged pit bulls, is the best lesson I've learned on this ride, so far.

Part 1
Great Places &
Memorable Rides

ODE TO A ROAD

*What makes a road great? Dramatic scenery,
scarce traffic and demanding curves are a
start. But destinations matter, too.*

What makes a particular road a great motorcycle road? If it were nothing more than the characteristics of the road itself, then the world would have few contenders indeed.

Some sport riders, asked to choose the "best" road, might pick a famed stretch of curves, such as U.S. 129 on the Tennessee-North Carolina border, a.k.a. Deals Gap, a.k.a. Tail of the Dragon. Lots of riders have crossed several states to sample its reputed 318 curves in eleven miles and have the T-shirt to prove it. Lots more would suggest that the level of squidly and sometimes dangerous riding, along with the intense law enforcement attention it has drawn, has done a lot to reduce the appeal of Deals Gap. Those riders might argue that the best pure road is no road at all, but a race track. Sport-touring riders, asked to choose the "best" road would probably list some names that combine challenging curves with a stunning setting, such as the Beartooth Highway high in the mountains on the Montana-Wyoming border or the Passo dello Stelvio in the Italian Alps. Laid-back cruising types might pick a scenic, linear National Park like the Blue Ridge Parkway, and never voice a complaint about its 45 mph speed limit. For adventure-touring types, it might be the North Yungas Road in Bolivia, known to locals as *El Camino de la Muerte* (The Road of Death) and to most of the rest of us as "the world's most dangerous road," a narrow, unpaved ledge carved into cliffs in the Andes by Paraguayan prisoners in the 1930s and the site of hundreds of fatalities every year. Just looking at photos of it can make you nervous. Saying you survived it gives you serious cred in the adventure-touring world. And then for the serious off-road riders, the ones who shun pavement altogether and avoid even dirt roads when possible, the best road is no road at all. It's a single-track trail, preferably far from all the traps and trappings of civilization.

But unless you ride a motorcycle in the cool, detached way a scientist conducts a laboratory experiment, totally separated from the world outside, there's far more to a great road than the road itself. Allow me to illustrate my point by telling you about one of my favorites, Ohio Route 555, a.k.a. the "Triple Nickel." There's no doubt 555 is a fun road, but to be honest, for the first seven years I lived in Ohio I avoided it. Some of my friends raved about it and I knew that riders from flatter parts of the state, such as the Cleveland area, would head south for long day rides in search of curves and they typically included 555.

The hype (or at least what I saw as hype) actually kept me away. I know from experience that when a road gets a reputation and draws out-of-town sport riders, there will always be some irresponsible elements in the group, which tends to lead to resentment among local residents and possibly a law enforcement crackdown. Both tend to trap responsible and irresponsible riders in the same web.

Since my initial aversion, however, 555 has gone from a road I had ridden just once, mainly to see firsthand what the fuss was about, to one of my favorites. What changed? I moved. And therein lies one of the keys to my personal answer to the question about what makes a road great. To me, greatness is not something judged merely by the number of curves or scenic views. A great road is one that has all that while also taking you to a place where you really want to be. That may seem like an absurdly simple concept, but it's the crucial difference between theoretical greatness and real-life greatness.

You see, I'll probably never make it to the North Yungas Road, but there are lots of roads I not only can ride, but need to ride. One of my favorite motorcycling games is to seek out ever more enjoyable routes to get from where I am to the places I need to get to on a regular basis, and since I moved, 555 is now an alternative route between my home and the small town on the banks of the Ohio River in West Virginia where I was born and raised, and where my parents still live. The most direct route between those two points is about 125 miles, and it's not a bad one. Almost all of it is two-lane and parts of it make for very pleasant riding, but there's also one small city with an excess of one-way streets and stoplights and a dozen depressed and tiny little towns that are big enough to slow me down but not sufficiently thriving to offer useful services or even a diverting view. The alternative involving 555 is about 150 miles, and it forces me to endure about thirty miles of boring four-lane. But it also includes the full length of this winding state route, from the south side of the small city of Zanesville to its dead end at Ohio Route 7. In between, there's really no such thing as a straight stretch, and although there are several tiny towns along the way (Portersville, Ringgold, Chesterhill, and Bartlett), there's not a single stoplight on the entire length of Route 555.

But that's just the beginning of what makes it my version of a fun ride.

If you're looking for a pleasant little road with meandering curves that will allow you to let your mind wander, shop else-where. Above all, 555 is a road that demands respect, and I ap-preciate that. Along most of it, shoulders are non-existent. This is a road that does not know forgiveness. Crossing the white line means losing the front wheel in four inches of crumbled asphalt and gravel, followed by a quick tumble into a ditch, or hard into a bank bordering a farmer's field, or skidding down a slope into a wooded ravine.

Along with respect, 555 demands your attention. At any given moment along its sixty-four miles you may well find the following:

A horse-drawn Amish buggy or a quarter-million-dollar piece of farm equipment, both moving at about the same speed, roughly 15 mph, and possibly lurking just beyond one of those many blind crests.

Several dozen curves splattered with an insignificant smat-tering of gravel, interspersed at unpredictable intervals with curves covered in a thick layer of gravel that has been kicked away only in the narrow wheel paths cleared by car tires. Let yourself be lulled into complacency by the former, and you may not be prepared to thread the needle when you suddenly encounter the latter.

Just beyond yet another blind crest, a ninety-degree curve, labeled 15 mph by the state, in a spot where there's no good topographical reason for you to expect a ninety-degree curve. It's only there out of respect for the property lines of a farmer's cornfield those many decades ago when the road was built.

A doe and her fawn crossing the road, even in the middle of the day in mid-summer, when by all rights they should be hidden away in the forest.

Miles of perfectly smooth pavement, followed by miles of frost-heaved, hastily patched, uneven asphalt. In spots, the earth has shifted underneath the road, allowing the pavement suddenly to drop three inches. If you come around a curve at full lean and find one of these settled areas in your line, your front wheel will be airborne for a second or so and I wish you well in achieving a happy landing.

Curves of every possible description, with no way of knowing what the next one will look like. Charge into the apex at 10/10ths and you may find that you've hopelessly overcooked a decreasing-radius corner. At that point, you're on your own, pilgrim. I can offer no further help.

These are the reasons I say Route 555 demands respect and attention. It provides little margin for error, so I provide my own. There's no other intelligent way to ride the Triple Nickel.

One day, I came upon a rider on a BMW R1200GS who had misjudged one of 555's endless turns. He was standing beside his downed motorcycle, forlorn but unhurt, and extremely lucky, if you ask me. His bike had slid down three feet of a steep and grassy slope without flipping or tumbling, and he was able to ride away after his buddies realized he was no longer back there, came to find him, and helped him drag the bike back to the roadway.

"The last time I did this, I was in Kazakhstan," he said, which proves the old truism that it's just as easy to crash close to home as it is on a certified "adventure."

Route 555 is not merely a hazardous workout of a ride, however. Along the way, it serves up farmland and woodland views, those few small single-stop-sign towns, and very little traffic. And the sheer variety of the road, with ridgetop sweepers, hairpins, decreasing-radius corners and ninety-degree turns around farm fields means you can't get bored unless it turns out you were really meant to be driving an Accord. Yes, it's quite likely in this countryside that you may come up behind an elderly woman in her sedan driving sedately to the church meeting, in addition to the slow-moving farm equipment and occasional horse-drawn buggy. With all those curves, you may need some patience to wait for a place to pass in a courteous way (and I try to keep in mind that what feels like a safe and easy pass to me can also look like a hairball move to a slow-moving car driver—not to mention an Amish buggy driver—who has no idea of the acceleration and braking abilities of a modern motorcycle). But 555 offers such an endless wealth of good riding that you can afford to have patience. You won't miss enjoying the good part while stuck behind the pokey Crown Victoria. All of it is the good part, and the locals don't drive very far.

And then there's that one additional essential ingredient that puts 555 on my personal list of great roads: It gets me somewhere I really want to be. Some people look at the odometers on my motorcycles and then are surprised when I tell them that I hardly ever get on a motorcycle for purely recreational purposes. I ride to get just about everywhere I need to go, be it to the local dealership for an oil filter, to the barber shop for a haircut, or to the office every day, back when I used to work in one. I ride to travel and to experience new places and see people I miss, but I nearly always have a destination, in addition to the best possible route that gets me there. I virtually never leave home, ride around a while and end up back home, with no more purpose than to enjoy the sensations of riding. I prefer a ride that has someone or someplace special waiting for me at the end. The ride feels better with a purpose.

Now I'm also honest enough with myself to admit that some of my reasons (okay, maybe even excuses) for the ride are pretty flimsy and wouldn't hold up to serious cross-examination. Do I really need another track day? Well, it does keep my skills (to the extent I have skills) honed a little more sharply and that keeps me safer on the road. After a long Ohio winter, deprived of rides of any distance, it doesn't take much to convince me to visit some family who live in the mountains of West Virginia, where some of the best riding in the east can be found, or in Maine, which provides all sort of interesting multi-day routing options. And, of course, it's only right that as a good son I check in on my parents now and then, so I make the trip down 555 to my former hometown.

And beyond its diabolical curves and country views and scarcity of traffic, that's what puts Route 555 on my personal list of great roads: what's waiting at the end. The best news in all of this? We don't have to go to Italy or Bolivia or even Wyoming to ride a great road. Any road that takes you toward someone or someplace special has the chance to have a little bit of greatness in it. Just pick the best one that gets you there. I'd personally recommend one like Route 555.

THE PATRON SAINT
OF ROADS

*The Columbia River Gorge is a spectacular
motorcycle destination on its own. But when
you dig into some of its oddities, you find that
we road riders owe a word of thanks to an
eccentric character named Sam Hill.*

In motorcycle photography terms, the Rowena Curves are a
cheap shot. Frankly, it's too easy to get a great riding photo
there. Just perch yourself along the edge of the cliff at the hilltop overlook and wait for the motorcycles to go by on the 180-
degree turns beneath you. You won't have to wait long, because
riders come from all over to enjoy the Rowena Curves, but
while you're waiting for the next shot you can enjoy expansive
views of the Columbia River while the cool wind sweeping
across the broad river valley refreshes you. There's a reason this

particular view has been on the cover of a book about motor-cycling in the Northwest, has been featured in uncounted magazines, and has shown up on television car commercials. Go ahead. Grab a great photo. I did. It's easy.

And just to the west of the Rowena Curves, on the old Columbia River Highway, you can also fill up your camera with images of the great falls in the gorge. Multnomah Falls, just one of several along the old river road, spears downward 620 feet as its water aims for the Columbia. The beauty of the river and the series of falls along the gorge were among the reasons this old road was built, decades before Interstate 84 slashed through the valley and gave people a faster way, bypassing all this beauty.

There's another stretch of asphalt nearby that's stranger and perhaps even more fun to ride than the Rowena Curves: 3.6 miles, twenty-five curves, leading to absolutely nothing. Imagine building your own private road for the purpose of sport riding. What would you build? Well, you'd probably start with a hillside location that would provide lots of opportunities for elevation change and curves, but would be open enough to allow generous sight lines. You'd make sure the asphalt was perfectly smooth and grippy, and you'd probably make each curve unique, designing a smorgasbord of hairpins, sweepers, increasing-radius, constant-radius and decreasing-radius turns. And you wouldn't waste space on a straight. Sport riding is about leaning, so the run would consist of turns, all the way.

That perfectly describes the Maryhill Loops.

What do all these roads have in common? Two things. They're among the attractions of the Columbia River Valley, which is a fine place to ride a motorcycle, and they all owe their existence to a guy named Sam Hill. Motorcycling isn't a religion, though some people approach it as one. If it were, street riders might light a candle now and then to Sam Hill, who could be considered the patron saint of good roads, a cause to which Hill, one of the founders of the Washington State Good Roads Association, dedicated himself with truly evangelical zeal. Of course his idea of a "good road" in 1899 was a little different from what a twenty-first-century rider of a sport-touring motorcycle might have in mind, but Hill still managed to leave as a legacy some very fine riding, even if that was not his intention.

Sam Hill was born a Quaker in North Carolina in 1857 but after the Civil War his family moved to Minneapolis, where he began the first of many chapters of his business career at the Great Northern Railway, eventually becoming a protégé of the railroad's owner and marrying his eldest daughter. Hill was a tireless spinner of dreams, however, and being a wealthy investor and a comfortable railroad executive in Minneapolis was not enough to satisfy him. He moved to Seattle, where among other ventures, he took over the local gas and lighting company. Over the years, Hill made and lost fortunes more than once with his entrepreneurial schemes and investments. He was a restless man bubbling over with ideas, and in the northwestern United States in the late nineteenth century, when few roads were even graded, much less paved, one of Hill's most persistent ideas was that building good roads could transform society. Good roads would let farmers get their produce to towns and railroads so they could make a decent profit. He believed roads would change society, encouraging young people to remain in the country, which he believed was a healthier place to be, instead of flocking to cities in search of a better life but often finding urban woes, instead.

"Good roads are more than my hobby, they are my religion," Hill once said, and he lived up to that claim. The Good Roads Association he led lobbied the Washington state government to build better roads, and Hill put $100,000 of his own money into his conviction. He built the Maryhill Loops, originally ten miles of privately built road on his own land, to test different methods of road construction and paving, and then paid for the entire Oregon legislature and the governor to come see it. Just as Hill's business interests proved more successful in Portland than Seattle, his pro-roads lobbying efforts also paid off in Oregon more than they ever did in Washington. At Hill's urging, the state began building the Columbia River Highway in 1913, making the gorge's river views, waterfalls and cliffs accessible to the growing number of automobiles and motorcycles on the roads. Portions of that same highway still carry thousands of people to the famed waterfalls today. Keep going east (on U.S. 30) and you'll reach the Rowena Curves, after leaving most of the sightseers behind.

As an easterner, I made my first, long-overdue visit to the Columbia River Gorge several years ago to attend Sportbike Northwest, a then-new rally sponsored by the online magazine *SoundRider!*, catering to riders of sportbikes and sport-touring bikes. Tom Mehren, founder of both the magazine and the rally, has a bit of Sam Hill's zeal in him, but Tom's enthusiasm centers on motorcycles and the people who ride them. In the years since I first traveled west for that early edition of Sportbike Northwest, Tom has expanded it into a series of rallies aimed at providing the perfect gathering and riding experience for owners of sportbikes, sport-touring machines, dual-sports and even scooters—all the motorcycling populations he felt were underserved in a country full of events catering to riders of cruisers and touring bikes. The difference between one of Tom's rallies and the big mega-rallies elsewhere can be summed up in a sentence: At Sportbike Northwest and its cousins, you'll find a lot less shopping available and a lot more options for the kind of riding you like to do.

The Columbia River Valley makes an excellent site for such an event, and Tom knows all the hidden roads worth riding. The routes laid out for the rally attendees included everything from the old river highway past those famous waterfalls to obscure numbered forest roads that suddenly rewarded me with an unexpected view of Mount Hood, glowing white in the summer sunshine, spotted through a break in the trees. And, of course, the famous Rowena Curves, not to mention a dozen other hilltop views of the Columbia rolling toward the sea.

On the second day of Sportbike Northwest, I decided to tag along with Tom and some of his other volunteers who were setting up the checkpoints for the day's poker run. Naturally, any poker run laid out by the *SoundRider!* crew is longer, curvier, and a little more demanding than your typical poker run. As we rode east on Route 14, we spotted two of Sam Hill's stranger projects, which were not among his most successful. Like everywhere else in western Oregon and Washington, heading east away from the coast, the landscape transitions from the wet, green coastline to brown hills and eventually to desert— and the temperature rises accordingly. On a warm summer day, you might think you're hallucinating from the rising heat when you see what appears to be Stonehenge off to the side. Hill built the concrete replica as an anti-war statement, demonstrating his disgust with the loss of life in World War I. Nearly as improbable as the Stonehenge replica is the huge mansion reposed at the roadside, seemingly in the middle of nowhere. No, you're not dreaming, but Sam Hill was. One of his big plans was to create a utopian farming community, true to his Quaker roots. He started by buying up 7,000 acres of land on the north bank of the Columbia and building a huge mansion for himself on the hillside overlooking the river. Hill had trouble attracting settlers to his planned utopia of Maryhill, however. Not many wanted to try to farm land that received less than a foot of rainfall a year. The utopia never materialized and Hill never lived in his mansion. Instead, it became an art museum that's still in operation today.

Tom and I weren't in Maryhill for a tour of the art gallery, however. We came here for the Maryhill Loops. Today, 3.6 miles of the original ten miles of Sam Hill's old demonstration road are still around, but they're impeccably maintained miles. Better yet, Tom rents the road during the rally and anyone who's registered can ride it as many times as desired. In fact, one of the poker run checkpoints is at the end of the Loops. We arrived early, so the road was still empty. I followed Tom as he rode his Yamaha FZ6 toward the entrance of the road. The volunteer working at the gate recognized him and let us pass before we could even come to a stop. Then, Tom waved me ahead with a broad sweep of his left hand. It was like the gesture of a man magnanimously offering me a gift, and as soon as it sank in, I accelerated past him and had the Maryhill Loops all to myself.

In an aerial view, the road looks like a very squiggly line drawn with a black marker on light brown paper. The dry, treeless slope allows for sightlines through most of the tight curves, which is always a good thing, though it mattered less than ever as I rode onto the Loops knowing that absolutely no other traffic lay ahead. I quickly dispensed with first gear and rolled into the series of curves in second, which would probably work for just about all of the road ahead. Shifting above third just amounts to putting unnecessary wear and tear on the gearshift lever, so I concentrated on rolling on and off the throttle, taking advantage of the grip provided by this dry, unmarred asphalt that has been lying here, curing in the sun. I scrubbed away the vestiges of chicken strips on my tires and soon, all too soon, I reached the gravel turnaround area at the top of the hill. The brief, 3.6-mile length is absolutely the only thing detracting from this ride. But when you can ride it again and again, as you can during the rally, even that isn't much of a drawback. And better yet, because I happened to get there early, I got to ride it alone.

I've ridden a number of race tracks that are faster, wider, and more varied. I've ridden roads that offer hundreds of miles of great curves, instead of less than four miles, and spectacular views instead of the brown hillsides of the Maryhill Loops. But I'm not sure I can remember a ride anywhere that was more concentrated into the essence of riding, without any distractions, with no traffic, no other riders coming up behind me, just me and the bike, the tires and the road melting together and sending their feedback to me through the suspension, and the total freedom to concentrate on nothing but that information, the power flowing from each turn of my wrist, and the braking from my two fingers on the lever. Nothing to experience but the ride itself.

I would not go so far as to call it a religious experience, but I neither would I consider it out of line to light a candle in homage of Sam Hill, patron saint of roads.

SLOW WAY AROUND

*A unique brand of camaraderie develops
when like-minded individuals take on a
challenge that's mystifying to the general
public, unappealing even to most fellow riders,
and requires the use of motorcycles
particularly ill-suited to the task.*

The throttle has been jammed to the stop for several minutes, the engine is screaming near 9,000 rpm and I'm tucked in tightly, desperately seeking every last mph of top speed as I flee Detroit on I-75 south. That's when the SUV in the left lane sedately passes me at about 75 mph. The kids in the back seat turn to stare at me, then point and laugh.

Glancing down at the gauges, I see the tach needle on the 1996 Suzuki GN125 start its slow descent once again and for the hundredth time I nervously check the mirrors for inattentive drivers coming up fast behind me. Dammit! The bike just won't stay above 60 mph in fifth gear on even the slightest up-hill grade.

At this point, you may reasonably ask what I'm doing on I-75 in Detroit, a city where everyone drives big cars at 80 mph, on a bike whose power output was once described by Iron Butt Rally commentator Bob Higdon as similar to a "hairdryer on wheels." You could blame my weakness for oddball motorcycle events, especially those that benefit a charitable cause. You could say it's because I'll do almost anything once if I get a story out of it. Personally, I prefer to blame Bill Murar. Yeah, that's it. It's Bill's fault.

Murar is a retired firefighter and paramedic with a special empathy for kids who have suffered burns. He also has an unnatural interest in small, underpowered motorcycles (even better if they're also old and rare). Once retired, he decided to combine those interests. He formed a foundation that supports medical assistance and recreational camps for pediatric burn victims, and fire safety training in the elementary schools. His first idea for raising funds was to get pledges by riding his vintage Sears Allstate scooter on a USA Four Corners Tour, a ride sanctioned by the Southern California Motorcycling Association. The Four Corners Tour involves visiting the four extremes of the contiguous United States (Madawaska, Maine; Key West, Florida; Blaine, Washington; and San Ysidro, California) on your motorcycle in a twenty-one-day period. Lots of people have done the Four Corners Tour, but attempting it on an antique scooter is another matter entirely. Already, you can see that Murar is no conventional thinker.

Five days into Murar's Four Corners Tour, his father died.

Later, the first Allstate blew up as he entered Key West city limits. He pulled his spare Allstate off his support vehicle and it imploded before he got out of Florida. He finally finished the ride, thanks to stubborn determination and his more trip-worthy Yamaha FZ1, then said, "Never again."

"It turned into a chore," Murar said, and he decided there had to be a better way to attract attention and donations for his foundation. That's when he invented the Lake Erie Loop.

The concept is simple. Ride one lap around Lake Erie, beginning and ending at a campground in northern Ohio that serves as Loop Headquarters, basically as fast as you can. What keeps this from becoming an international incident and a series of high-speed police pursuits through four U.S. states and one Canadian province are the three displacement classes, roughly 50cc, 125cc and 200cc, though vintage machines are allowed greater displacement. Given the size of the motorcycles, the Loop is more about persistence, endurance, reliability, and luck than about high speed. The first riders in each class to finish win cash prizes, but the winners generally donate the money back to Murar's foundation. Among hard-core Loopers, money is nothing compared to a cheap plastic trophy and a year's worth of bragging rights on the LEL Yahoo Group e-mail list.

Lured by the sheer oddity of the event, I mail in my entry for Lake Erie Loop V. I have no illusions of earning any of those bragging rights, but I can at least finish, right? In a lifetime of varied and sometimes-misguided motorcycling, I've done a thousand-mile day, I've survived the infamous and since revised Turn 12 at Road Atlanta, I've been caught on the road by unexpected snowfall, and sideswiped by a car at 60 mph on the freeway at 2 a.m. yet lived to tell those and other tales. I can surely survive the Loop. The only problem is, I don't have a Loop-legal motorcycle. Ah, but I know where I can get my hands on one.

Years ago, my father gave my mother a 1996 Suzuki GN125 as a fifty-ninth birthday present, knowing she wanted to get back into motorcycling and knowing she probably wouldn't spend the money on herself. She's since bought other bikes, but she'll always keep the GN125. As her phone is ringing, it dawns on me that it is Mother's Day. How am I going to phrase this? "Hi Mom. Say, I'd like to borrow your sentimental favorite motorcycle, flog it near redline for sixteen hours straight and possibly blow it to smoldering bits somewhere in Canada. Oh, by the way. Happy Mother's Day."

Fortunately for me, the concept of the Lake Erie Loop is just absurd enough that it's the sort of thing my mother couldn't resist. That's how I found myself on I-75 in Detroit on a Saturday evening on a twelve-year-old, air-cooled, 124cc tiddler, trying to avoid becoming just one more greasy spot between the bug splatters on the grill of a GMC Yukon. But wait, I'm getting ahead of myself.

When I first pull into the campground in northern Ohio that serves as event headquarters and start and finish lines, even a quick look around confirms that the serious Loopers prepare for this event all year. I've been studying up by reading the postings on the LEL Yahoo Group, but frankly, until you see, in the flesh, a 50cc Honda MB5 with a half-fairing torn off a Kawasaki racebike, an auxiliary fuel tank mounted on the tail, and both wooden-bead *and* sheepskin seat covers, the reality of commitment and innovation on display here just doesn't sink in. And that's just Murar's personal bike.

All kinds of motorcycles are pressed into service. Old

Honda CB200s and CL100s, vintage and modern scooters, a few random two-strokes. Many Loopers start with vintage machines to gain the displacement advantage allowed by the rules. Most add secondary or larger fuel tanks. Some load chase trucks with every conceivable spare part. By contrast, Eric Bechtol prides himself on not only riding his Aprilia Scarabeo scooter *in* the Loop, but also *to and from* the Loop, hauling all his camping gear. Probably the two extremes of LEL V were the motorcycles of Bobb Todd, a four-time Iron Butt Rally competitor from Canada who brought a not-available-in-the-USA liquid-cooled and fuel-injected Honda CBR125R, and Bob Uhl, who brought a homebuilt replica of a Whizzer, the only bike that was *pedaled* away from the starting line. The only thing all these motorcycles have in common is that none of them would be your first choice for a single-day ride around one of the Great Lakes.

Some competitors assemble chase truck crews which have become part of Loop legend. There was the year "Crazy Ken" Carlson threw an entire spare engine in his chase truck, just because he had it and, well, why not? When the original blew up near Buffalo, he swapped out the entire engine at roadside and finished. Then there was the year that Loop record-holder Ernie Copper couldn't understand why his borrowed 1972 Honda CB100 was handling so erratically until he noticed that the nut had vibrated off the swingarm pivot bolt, which was slowly working its way out. With no suitable nut available on the shoulder of the Ohio Turnpike, Copper and his chase crew drilled a hole in the bolt, inserted a cotter pin, and he blazed onward.

Such roadside innovations are now Loop lore.

Me, I know the only way I'll be featured in one of those oft-repeated tales is if I get really stupid or very unlucky. As we line up for the start, my two goals are to finish and not create a memorable and unpleasant family tale by blowing up my mother's motorcycle. As the field buzzes away from the starting line at 6 a.m. on a warm Saturday, I make my first mistake by choosing to circle the lake counterclockwise, thinking it will make it easier to navigate construction detours at the border crossing in Detroit. The more experienced Loopers choose the clockwise route. I won't discover why until later. But before I realize the folly of that mistake, I make a few smaller ones by missing a turn and going through a small Ohio town I should have bypassed, and getting off the New York State Thruway at the wrong exit, losing time at stoplights and in traffic while the veterans roll on without delay. Once I'm in the flat farmland of southern Ontario, I learn why everyone else runs the Loop clockwise. For more than 200 miles I battle a headwind, shifting back and forth between fourth and fifth gears, trying to balance my desire to maintain speed with my fear of hurling the GN125's connecting rod into the roadside tomato fields. Suddenly, my two modest goals seem incompatible. If I keep the little GN125 in fourth gear, I can maintain forward momentum against the headwind, but at 9,000 rpm, 90 percent of redline, I'm in constant fear of turning the engine into shrapnel. Shifting to fifth lowers the rpm to a less tortuous 7,500, but my speed keeps slipping and suddenly it feels like I'll never finish this damn loop. No wonder I'm the only one riding this direction.

By the time I've survived Detroit and crossed the state line into Ohio, night and my enthusiasm are falling rapidly. On the fly, I reach out and try to adjust the aim of the Suzuki's little five-inch headlight, but the effort is futile, and I learn to live with the anemic yellow smudge of light in the roadway ahead as I roll through the dark, deer-infested woods and fields of northern Ohio, butt burning, shoulders knotted and aching. It's that time of evening when even the mental image of a sleeping bag in a tent on the hard ground hovers in the mind like a nirvana of feathery pillows and Loopers peer deep into the abyss of the soul and ask themselves the central questions of life, such as, "Does that valve clatter sound like it's getting worse?" and "Why did I think this would be fun?"

I finally roll into the campground 16 hours and 36 minutes after I started. Ken Carlson has set a new class record on his Honda CL100, which runs in the 50cc class because of its vintage status, of 13:05. But the overall winner is Iron Butt veteran Bobb Todd, who finished in 10:58, still short of Ernie Copper's all-time record of 10:19. Proving again that the key to making time is not stopping, Todd completed the Loop with three gas stops and two border crossings that totaled forty-five minutes of non-moving time.

Basic math skills and a passing familiarity with traffic laws are probably enough to have you wondering about the legality of all this. Better not to think about it too much, I say. While I was never a contender, I can also say that the laws of physics and the realities of 1970s-era air-cooled engine technology and 124cc of displacement were far more effective at keeping me in check than any posted speed limit could have been.

And whatever happened to Bob Uhl's quixotic attempt to ride a Whizzer around Lake Erie? He made it as far as Toledo, where mechanical problems slowed him, then reality set in and turned him around. He left early, but rumor has it he vowed to return with a more Loop-ready motorcycle and less audacity.

Sounds like another Looper is born.

WHERE THE ROAD
AND THE SKY COLLIDE

No eight miles of pavement on this continent
puts you through bigger changes than the
Mount Washington Auto Road. Strange things
happen on the peak.

No other eight miles of road on this continent puts you through bigger changes than the Mount Washington Auto Road. That fact has little to do with the eight miles of horizontal movement, and everything to do with the 4,700 feet of vertical ascent.

Strange things happen on the peak of Mount Washington. At 6,288 feet, it is the highest point in New Hampshire and the third-highest east of the Mississippi, but those are not the numbers that distinguish it. The mountain's fame comes from its awful weather, not its size. The most famous of that awful weather happened in April, 1934, when storms over the Great Lakes and the Carolina coast, along with a high pressure ridge in eastern Canada, combined to create unusual pressure gradients. The three-man crew in the Mount Washington observatory at the time took their scientific duties seriously. Living in stone huts on the peak with several pet cats for company, they took measurements around the clock. At 4 a.m. the night of the infamous storm, one of the crew checked the anemometer and saw a reading of 105 mph. He could tell by the sound outside that the wind was stronger than that. The anemometer must have been icing up. In the nighttime darkness, he climbed the ladder to the rooftop equipment. All day long, thick fog had enveloped the peak and rime ice a foot thick had formed on surfaces. The crewman cracked off the ice buildup on the anemometer with a wooden club before retreating back inside. The winds kept building, and the next afternoon, the readings topped 200 mph several times. Then, one gust pushed the Mount Washington equipment to the highest wind speed ever recorded on the face of the earth: 231 mph. Later, the National Weather Service tested the anemometer, which had been specially built for Mount Washington, and confirmed its accuracy.

On the clearest of days, New York's Mount Marcy, the highest point two states away, can be seen from Mount Washington, and the Maine coast, sixty miles away, is easy to spot. Many winter days, visibility is measured in feet and eighty-pound chunks of ice are blown around by the wind, threatening the observatory staff making their hourly observations. The weather is milder in the summer. Usually. Then came July 20, 1996, when the wind speed *averaged* 100 mph for the day.

Mount Washington is often as snowy as mountains three times its height, as cold as polar regions, and is raked by winds that have no comparison, but there's one more fact that distinguishes it, one that makes it particularly relevant to those of us who ride. There's a road that goes to the peak, meaning even those of us who don't want to endure eight-day tours of twelve-hour shifts taking weather observations can get there. Even on our motorcycles, at least some of the time—weather permitting, of course. That road is the Mount Washington Auto Road.

Work first began on a road to the summit in 1855, but the project became so costly that the company building it went bankrupt the following year, after getting only about halfway up the eastern side of the mountain. Meanwhile, another entrepreneur hatched plans to build a cog railway on the western side of Mount Washington. More than 150 years later, you can still reach the top by either method. With a special motorcycle toll of $14 for a solo rider (plus $8 for a passenger), the Auto Road is the less-expensive and more-fun option. You can't take your motorcycle on the train.

With all this lore in mind, I turn off Route 16 at Glen House for a ride up the Auto Road on a perfect, midsummer New England day: a light breeze, temperatures in the low eighties, plenty of sunshine. As I stop to pay, the man working the toll booth tells me my timing is good, because the road had been closed to motorcycles earlier in the day. Overnight rains had left the unpaved sections muddy and slippery, and he warns me the road is undoubtedly still damp. I'm riding a Suzuki DL650 V-Strom, however, which is just about the perfect bike for handling roads that mix sections of asphalt with stretches of dirt. As I hand over my money, I read the sign reporting the conditions at the peak: fifty-three degrees with 40 mph winds.

That constitutes fine summer weather for the top of Mount Washington and I'm beginning to think this ride could offer a little less drama than expected. Could it be that I'm about to ride to the spot that advertises itself as the "Home of the World's Worst Weather" and come away disappointed? Yawning even? Then it gets worse. As I begin climbing through the wooded lower slopes of the mountain, a guy on a Harley passes me on his way down. He's wearing shorts. Shorts?! What happened to the death-defying weather? Is this going to be just another road? No matter, now. I've paid my toll, so up I go.

Mile markers along the road report on my vertical progress. When I reach the sign announcing 4,000 feet elevation, I feel the first gusts of wind. A little farther on, the pavement gives way to packed dirt. At the lower elevations, I was riding through a pleasant New England forest, but as I climb the mountain along Chandler Ridge, the trees become smaller and fewer, and as I reach the sign marking 5,000 feet, I leave behind the last stunted trees. Now, the views open up, and when I take my eyes off the road for a second, I see blue mountains filing off into the distance. Closer to my path, clumpy grass and boulders covered with lichens stud the steep slopes alongside the narrow road. As the road criss-crosses the mountainside, I round a curve and suddenly the wind, previously blocked by the massive bulk of the mountain, is free to slam into me like a rogue wave. At once, the road looks even narrower than it did before, as the buffeting crosswind tries to push me sideways on the dirt road into the path of oncoming traffic. Remember how I said the V-Strom was the perfect bike for a little bit of dirt-road climbing? What was I thinking? Have you seen the surface area of the fairing on this thing? Christopher Columbus would have envied sails that big when he crossed the Atlantic.

With the wind trying to kill me, I fold myself into a full racer's tuck, trying to minimize my profile, even though I'm just crawling up the slope at 25 mph in first gear. Clearly, I'm going to need a lot more training and skills before I enter the Pikes Peak International Hill Climb. For now, I'm just reminding myself not to keep a death grip on the handlebar, which will only magnify unwanted steering inputs from every gust grabbing at my elbows, and I'm focused on holding my line. With the wind pushing me into the mountain, the temptation is to lean the other way, but that means leaning toward the roadside abyss. I imagine the gale stopping suddenly and my lean steering me right over the edge of the road, sending me tumbling down that steep boulder field, smashing my ribs against granite stones in an uncontrolled 500-foot descent, all under the horrified gaze of little kids in a minivan who will need years of therapy to erase the horrible images of their family trip to Mount Washington. Then, as my hyperactive imagination plays out these scenarios, I round another hairpin, the pavement resumes, and once again I am sheltered from the wind in a fold of the mountain. I suddenly find that riding a motorcycle is easy again, just like it usually is, and I pull uneventfully into the parking lot near the summit.

A cluster of buildings at the top of Mount Washington mixes old and new. Among the oldest is the Tip Top House, a stone structure built in the 1850s as a small hotel for people who journeyed to the top even before the Cog Railway or the Auto Road were completed. Also atop the highest point in New England are communications and television towers, and, of course, the Mount Washington Observatory, where weather observations are still carefully recorded and scientific research conducted. The absolute top of the summit is reached by steps that lead to a pile of rocks and a surprisingly rustic wooden sign that marks the peak. Visitors pose next to the sign, the wind tearing at their hair and the jackets they hastily put on when they got out of their cars and felt the thirty-degree difference from down below.

The wind is even stronger on the rooftop platform of the observatory. The stone building juts out from the mountain's edge, catching the full flow of the winds. This platform is the testing ground for an unofficial designation called membership in the Century Club. To get into the Century Club, you have to walk one lap of the platform in winds of at least 100 mph without falling down or holding on to anything. What makes this even harder is that you'll probably be walking on rime ice, which is the name for fog droplets that freeze on contact with any exposed surface in the cold winter months. On my visit, I'm nowhere near qualifying for the Century Club, but the wind is strong enough that I can lean into it twenty degrees off vertical with no danger of falling. There's plenty of cold, relentless airflow to hold me up. I've been through enough hurricanes that I have to stop and think before I can tell you the precise number. But the wind on Mount Washington felt just as strong. That sign at the bottom saying the winds at the peak are 40 mph is in need of updating, I'm convinced, as I take in the views from this rocky spot where, in the words from an old song, "the road and the sky collide." On Mount Washington, more than most places in this part of the world, I truly feel that I'm perched on a rock, scraping the sky, nearer the empty chill of space.

I linger at the top, and then linger a bit more, thinking about going back down that muddy ledge where the wind tried to rip me off the mountain's flank like wolf scratching off an annoying flea. As it turns out, however, the wind has shifted directions again, and I ride down Chandler Ridge without ever having to battle so much as a single nasty gust. Looking back, my fears that my anticipation of riding to the peak would end in disappointment were both fulfilled and unfounded. It is just a road, one that like any other should be ridden at a pace suitable for the conditions. But in the end it wasn't just another ride, it was a ride to one of those places where day-to-day events are far from what we consider ordinary. The kinds of places we don't experience often. Reaching those special places is not the reason we ride most days, but it's the reason we remember certain days the most.

RUINS

A civilization from a thousand years ago and one eccentric man's obsession from twenty-five years ago bookend a journey to east-central Mexico.

I was thousands of miles into my trip, and just three miles from the last and strangest destination on my list of places to visit in east-central Mexico, when my motorcycle and I disappeared into a cloud. As I rode into the little mountain town of Xilitla, the rising road and the lowering clouds finally met and swallowed me in cool mist.

Cool mist was not what I'd longed for when I planned a December trip to Mexico.

Instead, after living for thirteen years in locations where snow was a meteorological impossibility, followed by several years of Ohio winters, I craved an escape from the gray dreariness of a Midwest December and a taste of nothing more complicated than the feel of warm, moist, tropical air flowing under the chinbar of my helmet. I had been planning the Mexico trip for months, and even bought the right motorcycle for the trip a year in advance when I found a deal I couldn't pass up on a BMW F650, one of the few motorcycles that works well on both a U.S. interstate (or an equally smooth Mexican *cuota*, or toll road) and on a formerly paved, muddy, rock-studded shortcut, as I would confirm firsthand on my way to Xilitla.

While the rejuvenating feeling of tropical warmth might have been enough to satisfy me, any journey needs a destination, if only to justify the trip to ourselves and those left at home. My bookend destinations were two sets of ruins, one ancient and one modern. The ancient was El Tajín. More than a thousand years ago, it was the most important city on the Gulf coast, built by the Totonac people. It was abandoned by the time the Spanish arrived. Even today, only a fraction of the 150 or so buildings here have been excavated. The most interesting discoveries so far, at least for a non-archaeologist such as myself, are the Pyramid of the Niches, a building-sized calendar with 365 cubbyhole recesses with figures carved into the stone, and the etchings on the stones around the ceremonial ball court, some of which appear to show human sacrifices. Historians still wonder: who got the knife? The winners of the game or the losers? Keep in mind, being sacrificed to the gods was considered by some cultures to be a great honor.

I rode into the nearly empty grounds of El Tajín on the sunniest day of my trip, with the luxury of a full afternoon to walk through the ancient city, now grassy and silent. Two hedges of flowering *amapola* bushes created a tunnel entrance into the grounds, where the few visitors, both foreign and Mexican, wandered uncrowded while old women worked silently at cleaning moss and lichens from the stones of the buildings to preserve them. For me, one of the rarest and most coveted feelings on any motorcycle ride is the luxury of free time. Typically, especially at home, my rides and trips are accompanied by a small black cloud that only I can see, a nagging feeling deep in the background of my mind that I soon need to be somewhere else, that someone is waiting for me, or that dawdling means neglecting other duties. That afternoon at El Tajín was the turnaround point in my trip. I had no farther to go that day, my hotel room for the night was already secured (the same one as the previous night), and nobody was expecting me to be anywhere else. That alone, that opportunity to relax on a grassy slope among ancient monuments after a 2,000-mile dash southward, was among the most savored parts of my afternoon amidst the ruins.

I tipped the self-appointed parking lot attendant (who promised me he had watched my motorcycle carefully) at El Tajín and started back toward the city where I was staying for the night. I abandoned the speedy, empty toll road, choosing narrow side roads through towns with nearly as many syllables in their names as residents in their little houses: Praxedis Guerrero, Manlio Fabio Altamirano. It was the trip's best day of riding, not because of anything special about the roads I was riding, but rather thanks to the sunshine, the warmth, and the lack of the kind of schedule one has to stick to in order to cross several U.S. and Mexican states and be back home in less than two weeks.

The next day, unfortunately it was time to aim north. After my afternoon of sun at El Tajín, the weather showed no further compassion for how far I'd come in search of a tropical breeze. The winds turned from the north and thick clouds obscured the sun as I rode west into the mountains to the little town of Xilitla and *la casa del inglés*, the second set of ruins on my itinerary, the modern ruins, even stranger than El Tajín. The main roads would have taken me there in an inefficient zig-zag pattern, but a small yellow line on my Guia Roji map, connecting the little crossroads of San Sebastián and the small city of Huejutla de Reyes, suggested itself as a shortcut that could shave fifty miles off the trip, giving me more time to explore *la casa del inglés*. By the time I reached San Sebastián, however, a light drizzle was falling, and within a few miles, my shortcut offered a new set of challenges.

It appeared the road had been paved at some point, but now it consisted of hard-packed mud, turned slick by the light rain and studded with softball-sized stones and shards of old asphalt, long since shattered by the pounding of the dump trucks that wallowed through the lunar-class potholes on their way to a local quarry. Following the trucks meant riding so slowly I was lugging the engine even in first gear, while gradually being coated with the mud they added to the misty rain. Passing them meant trying to squeeze by the lumbering beasts on the slick and narrow road, wondering if at any moment they might change course to avoid the worst of the potholes and force me into the ditch. I finally reached pavement at the edge of Huejutla de Reyes with the suspicion that my shortcut had saved me fifty miles of distance and five minutes of travel time.

I picked my way through the narrow city streets, trying not to lose the thread of the route leading toward Tamazunchale, trying not to lose the tires' tenuous grip on the greasy wet pavement, until a young policeman halted all traffic at an intersection. Sitting at the front of the line of stopped cars, I had a perfect view of a Christmas procession as locals on foot carried figures of saints to the church. Plodding along in the drizzle, the procession was more mournful, or at least respectful, than festive. This is the difference that travel makes: On a trip back home, I'd be annoyed to be stopped because of a parade, fuming about where I needed to be. Here, nearly two thousand miles from home, I was just pleased to have a front-row view. That, for me at least, is the transforming magic of foreign surroundings. The ordinary can become memorable, and even mundane tasks become learning experiences. An inconvenience becomes an opportunity to peer into other lives.

Taking advantage of the wait, I decided to quiz the policeman and try to learn if the road ahead was as bad as the one that brought me to Huejutla de Reyes.

"*¿Cómo está el camino a Tamazunchale? ¿Está en malas condiciones?*" I asked.

The young policeman shrugged and smiled self-consciously. "*No sé*," he replied. "*Nunca he ido.*" He didn't know what the road was like. He'd never been to Tamazunchale, the closest city bigger than his own and just thirty miles away. That fact suggested to me that he'd never left his home town.

In Tamazunchale, I was delayed again by a Christmas procession, one that was far less enjoyable than even the dour parade in Huejutla de Reyes. Two trucks belched diesel smoke as they labored through narrow streets built ages ago for pedestrians and horses. Struggling to make their way around sharp corners and past parked cars, the trucks carried Christmas decorations both secular and religious, from the statue of the Virgin Mary and child to a huge evergreen, all of it destined to adorn the town's central plaza. When finally I escaped the snarled traffic of Tamazunchale, I spiraled upward until I rode into the clouds near *la casa del inglés*, the most other-worldly ruins I've seen yet.

An Englishman, Edward James—heir to a fortune, a patron of surrealist art, and rumored by some to be the illegitimate son of King Edward VII—came to Mexico in the 1950s on the sort of whimsical venture that characterized his life: He planned to grow orchids in the moist mountain valley. When a rare frost wiped out the flowers, James began building a garden of concrete, instead. He dreamed up designs and local workers made wooden forms and cast his fancies in concrete. The work continued for more than a decade, until James died in 1984. James called the place Las Pozas, or the pools, for the many pools and waterfalls in the stream that runs through it. Locals just referred to it as *la casa del inglés*, the house of the Englishman. It's a place not known by a lot of people outside of its part of Mexico, but I occasionally run into a motorcyclist who has been there. The sheer strangeness of Las Pozas and the good riding in the Sierra Madre Oriental Mountains around it, draw riders.

I rode down the driveway of packed mud studded with fist-sized rocks that led to the entrance to Las Pozas, negotiating yet one more obstacle on this long and slippery day without dumping the BMW. Then I paid my modest entrance fee and began exploring one man's surrealistic vision of Eden.

The clouds still swirled around me, not above, making this strangest of places look even more like an improbable late-night dream. Winding paths led through the jungle to both natural and manmade pools in the tumbling stream. Huge concrete flowers sprouted alongside trails. Giant petals adorned highly styled bridges. Spiral stairs rose to mid-air, leading to nothing. I could have spent hours exploring those pathways that took years to build. I still wouldn't have found all the concrete secrets the eccentric Englishman tucked away in the jungle. But the afternoon was already turning dark, especially in the belly of the cloud, and I still had miles to go before I slept.

My last impression of Las Pozas was how relentlessly the jungle was encroaching, day by day reclaiming, with each clinging vine and each crack-splitting root, the work built over decades. It seemed inevitable, as I rode away from those strangest of modern-day ruins, that Edward James's odd structures would be swallowed up. I left wondering if, ten centuries from now, someone would dig up Las Pozas, as we now recover El Tajín. If so, what would they make of it?

There has since been a postscript to the story, however. In 2007, Las Pozas was acquired by a non-profit organization called Fondo Xilitla, which was created by a Mexican charitable foundation with support from the state government and, appropriately enough, from CEMEX, the huge Mexican cement and infrastructure company. Maybe *la casa del inglés* will still be there many years from now, giving me a good excuse to return to Mexico's mountain valleys. If I never make it back, I'll always be grateful I saw it when I did. Even if the clouds obscured my view and the balmy days during my trip were fewer than I'd hoped for, I try always to remember the many reasons I have to feel fortunate. Riding toward home, it dawned on me that I'd seen more of Mexico in a few days than that young policeman in Huejutla de Reyes had seen in his lifetime. Reason to be grateful, indeed.

BURRITOS TO DIE FOR

If I died on that lonely, West Texas road,
nobody would know that my own stubbornness
and a plate of burritos were to blame.

As a former newspaper reporter, I could easily imagine the item that would appear in the weekly paper in Marfa, Texas. It would probably be just a couple of inches buried on an inside page.

Coroner Tries to Identify Motorcyclist Fried by Lightning on U.S. 90

The county coroner has yet to identify the crispy remains of a motorcyclist struck by lightning earlier this week on U.S. 90 between Marfa and Van Horn. The sheriff's department is also checking motor vehicle records to see if the brand new Harley-Davidson Road King with California manufacturer plates that was ridden by the deceased was stolen.

As a record of my final living moments on this earth, it

wouldn't be much. And there'd be no witness to tell the full story: that I'd died on that lonely plain in West Texas due to my own stubborn nature and a plate of bean burritos.

It was late afternoon on a warm September day and I'd wrapped up the exploring and photography for a magazine story about Big Bend National Park and the surrounding area. It had been a fun few days, riding the rolling River Road between the dusty Texas border town of Presidio and the western edge of the park, swerving to avoid the tarantulas that occasionally scuttle across the road in their single-minded search for a mate (it's breeding season) and hiking to the remains of the Homer Wilson Ranch, catching a breather in the scrap of shade from its thick stone walls, and, in its enveloping silence, imagining the loneliness of the homesteaders who scratched out a living in this remote and arid site. Big Bend has always been the kind of place most humans consider desolate. The first Spanish explorers who came through this area labeled it "*la tierra despoblada,*" the uninhabited land, decided it was empty of humans for good reason, and continued onward in their search for cities of gold that they could more easily plunder. Today, Big Bend has a few paved roads, a hotel, maintained trails, five visitors centers and other amenities of a U.S. National Park. But most of the park's 800,000 acres are still empty, unmolested *tierra despoblada,* the kind of place where the foolish can and do still get lost and die of thirst, or set up camp in the wrong spot at the wrong time and get swept away in a flash flood, or come across a mountain lion on a remote trail very, very far from help, should help be needed. Big Bend is a stark and beautiful landscape where on any given evening the temperature on the peaks of the Chisos Mountains might be thirty degrees cooler than on the sweltering banks of the Rio Grande below. In other words, it is one of those great unique places on earth well worth a visit.

All fine explorations must eventually come to an end, however, and other duties required my presence in San Diego, 1,100 miles away, in less than forty-eight hours. Plus, heavy-looking clouds, nurtured by the afternoon heat, were sailing in across the Mexican border, threatening an unsettled and unpredictable end to the day. One such storm had already chased me into the park's Panther Junction Visitors Center, where I examined the displays while the deluge flooded the road and the parking area outside. More such downpours appeared inevitable and clearly it was time to put my borrowed Road King to use and cover some miles.

I rode north out of the park to the town of Marathon, where I picked up U.S. 90 and began angling west and north. When I reached the next town, Alpine, it was too soon to stop for the night, so I pressed on. At Marfa, the sun was still well above the horizon and I was mindful of the many miles between me and San Diego. I considered stopping anyway, and I considered pressing on for another hour or two. I could have flipped a coin. Instead, it was a plate of burritos that made the decision for me.

This particular plate of burritos had been recommended by the late Eddie James, a multi-time Iron Butt Rally competitor who worked for the Ride for Kids fundraisers and who was the motorcycling embodiment of the guy in that old Johnny Cash song, "I've Been Everywhere." I'm not a big football fan, and I've never traveled in Texas that much, so Eddie had to fill me in on the history of Chuy's Restaurant in Van Horn. Chuy's has been serving Mexican food on the dusty main street since 1959 and probably would have continued feeding the locals and the occasional traveler who wandered in off of I-10 in general obscurity if not for a chance visit in 1987. Former NFL coach and announcer John Madden, who's famously opposed to flying, was traveling through Texas on I-10 in his bus and needed a place to watch the football game. By chance he stopped at Chuy's, watched the game on the restaurant's TV, loved the food, and periodically plugged the restaurant afterward. That's the kind of national advertising a joint like that could never buy, so it's not surprising that the little restaurant in Van Horn is now something of a John Madden shrine, complete with a table reserved for him, should he happen to stop in again. He's been known to do so.

Chuy's works quite well for me, too. The food is good, the ambience friendly and unpretentious. Meanwhile, Van Horn, situated just off I-10 in a generally empty part of West Texas, has a surplus of motels along its main street, between the two interstate exits that bookend the town. Thus, lodging is plentiful and cheap. In other words, the town has all the ingredients I need when I'm on the road, have to cover some miles, and merely need food and shelter for the night. So with a recommendation from Eddie and an endorsement from John Madden, both big and enthusiastic guys, I'd stopped there on my way to Big Bend and had enjoyed a plate of burritos, rice and beans at Chuy's. Now, days later, as I rolled through Marfa on my way back west, that memory tipped the balance and convinced me to keep riding. Moments after making this decision, I cleared the edge of town, where a sign warned: NO SERVICES 73 MILES.

About ten miles into that lonely stretch, I saw the storms blooming ahead.

U.S. 90 cut a straight slash northwest through its portion of West Texas, the strip of asphalt flat and straight like a manmade line on a map. The flat, nearly featureless land allowed me to see much farther than an Easterner like me is accustomed to seeing. Far ahead, to the left of the road's trace to the horizon, a churning mass of dark clouds was building, another isolated thunderstorm moving in from the general direction of the border. Worse, another storm was building to the right. Between those two looming threats, dead ahead and above the strip of road that was my only company on that lonely plain, the sun shone down from a patch of blue sky as if to illuminate my path to burrito heaven.

Could I reach that opening before the storm clouds converged? Just how far away were the storms? In a foreign (to me) landscape devoid of markers that would help me judge the distances, I had no clue. Turning back held no allure (it almost never does), so my only choice was to roll on the throttle and turn the landscape's disadvantageous desolation into an advantage: There was no shelter out here, no place to find refuge should the storm catch me, but that also meant there was nothing to slow me down, no traffic or crossroads or impediments. I may have violated a few Texas traffic laws as I rumbled northwest on U.S. 90, hunched behind the Road King's windshield, chasing the narrowing gap between the clouds in what felt like slow motion. A few outer gusts from the twin storms grabbed at the big fork-mounted windscreen and jostled the bike while lightning flashed in the boiling clouds. I had what seemed like way too much time to think, and my mind went back to a magazine article I'd co-written not too long before, called "Worst Cases: What to Do When It All Goes Wrong." The first topic among those worst-case scenarios was getting caught in a lightning storm. About the only advice from the article that would apply out here was the last resort: Park the motorcycle, walk away from it, crouch down on the balls of your feet and hope for the best. It seemed like a thin hope to cling to.

As I came closer to the gap in the twin storms, and as that gap narrowed at about the same rate I approached, a few stray but lush drops of rain pelted the windshield and more gusts snatched at the big Harley. Then, as quickly as opening a door and stepping from a dim room into the bright light of day, I burst through the gap in those ominous clouds and rode into sunlight. I'd made it.

Some twenty miles later, I stepped off the bike and walked into the air conditioned office of a little motel in Van Horn. The sun was just setting, but the temperature was still near ninety degrees. A complaint about the excess of heat and the paucity of rain were the first words of greeting from the woman working behind the motel desk. I reported that I'd seen three thunderstorms that very day, and two of them had passed by less than twenty-five miles from Van Horn. Her silent look screamed skepticism.

War correspondents say there's a specific sort of thrill to the experience of being shot at and missed. Frankly, I'll be content if dodging West Texas lightning is as close as I come to the experience. In any case, the burritos at Chuy's tasted especially good that evening.

DROPPING THE DUCATI

*Did you hear about the guy who dropped the
only Ducati 999s Team USA replica in the
country? Crashed it on pit lane! No, really.*

Is there a statute of limitations on stupidity?

After enough time has passed, after the injuries have healed
and most others have forgotten our foolishness, we can, if we're
lucky, look back and laugh instead of wincing. For me, that
means I can tell you about the time I dropped the Ducati.

The day starts with promise. In the strong, angled sunlight
of an August morning, we gather around Sportbike Track Time
owner Monte Lutz for the riders meeting at the first-ever
Ducati Revs Ohio Day at the Mid-Ohio Sports Car Course. It's
a track I have seen several times as a race spectator, but, although it is the closest major track to my home at this time, I
have never ridden it. I am eagerly looking forward to changing
that. As I stand there anonymously among the track-day riders, listening to Monte run through the rules and procedures, I

hear one guy whisper to his buddy, "Lance Oliver of *Cycle World* is here to do a test ride." I chuckle inside but keep quiet. Actually, I've never written for *Cycle World*.

After the riders meeting, I look over the new Ducati Team USA replica that I'll be riding. Essentially, the Team USA bike is a street-legal 999s painted to look like the AMA Superbikes ridden in the 2006 season by Neil Hodgson and Ben Bostrom. Racers get paid to put sponsors' logos on their bikes. Slapping those stickers on your streetbike usually looks pretentious and vaguely embarrassing, like one of those front-wheel-drive import cars with a big rear wing bolted on the back. The Ducati is so racy looking, however, and the paint scheme is so well done, without being overdone, that the entire effect just looks right. On this bike, you could make a case that anything *other than* racebike paint would look out of place.

As I examine the 999s in the Mid-Ohio garage, Ducati regional rep Jason Chinnock walks up. "This is the only one of these in the country," he says, patting the shapely tail section of the 999s Team USA replica. "Have fun."

The only one, huh? That's something to think about as I wait for my first session on the track. And here's another thing to think about: the big sticker they gave me at registration with the letter "A" on it. "A" as in Advanced. Sportbike Track Time runs three groups: Novice, for first-timers on the track; Advanced, for those with racing experience; and Intermediate, to catch everyone in between. I've been to a few riding schools and have done my best to learn my way past an apex from the likes of Kevin Schwantz and Jason Pridmore, and I've done my share of track days. But a man's got to know his limitations, and I know mine. I'm an intermediate rider through and through.

Let's review: a borrowed and unfamiliar bike, a track I've

never ridden before, and hey, I'm no racer. Excuse me, but shouldn't I be in the intermediate group?

"Intermediate is full so we put you in Advanced," explains Lutz.

So, while the Intermediate group pulls onto the track without me for the first session, I try to pass the time profitably by familiarizing myself with the Team USA replica as I wait to be tossed onto Mid-Ohio with the sharks. As I examine the Ducati's gauges, however, I can't seem to find the odometer when I toggle through the digital display. This must be the tripmeter, I'm thinking, because it says 7.

"No, that's the odometer," says Aaron Bell, another Ducati rep also about to go on the track. Seven miles on the engine and I'm about to rev it to redline on the track? Apparently Ducati's not worried about break-in procedures. The mileage leads me to examine the tires more closely. Street tires, not track-day tires, and scrubbed in about as much as you can in seven miles, which is to say, not much. Then, on the very first lap by the Intermediate group ahead of us, a Suzuki blows its engine and oils down the long Mid-Ohio back straight, the one part of the track where you see the highest speeds and the hardest braking. The delay for the cleanup gives me more time to think. New bike, unscrubbed tires, oil on the track, and me, about to be unleashed in the midst of the Advanced riders.

I know what you're thinking: "He's in over his head. The dang fool is going to toss the only Team USA 999s in the *entire* United States."

Sadly, you'd be right.

But not yet.

The first lap, I'm following Aaron, who promises to show me some lines and ride a conservative pace until we get some heat in the tires. Riding into the keyhole turn at a just-getting-warmed-up pace, the new front tire pushes badly, giving me a good scare. Now, I can handle a little rear-tire slippage on the track, even enjoy it if it's progressive and controllable. But I prefer my front tire to feel like a sharp axe slicing into a tree trunk. Pure bite.

"Here it comes," you're thinking. "This is where he throws it into the gravel trap."

Not yet.

Half a lap later, the front pushes again, and in the interests of not crashing the innocent bike before it reaches double-digit mileage, I devote the rest of the first session to scrubbing in the tires at a moderate pace. The session is abbreviated due to the time lost to the oil spill cleanup, and for the first time in my life I'm actually glad to have fewer minutes on the track. It means none of the other riders in the Advanced group lap me.

The Ducati reps use their influence (after all, they're paying for the track) and score an "I" sticker for me so I can join the Intermediate group and go out again. The Intermediate pace is more my speed, and I separate myself from the heavier traffic of this group and start to get a feel for the bike. The Ducati's broad V-twin powerband makes life easy. If I'm off by one gear, coming out of a corner in third when I should be in second, the bike hardly cares. It just shrugs off my mistake and pulls me down the straight. After just two sessions, it's already time for the lunch break, thanks to the disruption of the schedule due to the long oil cleanup, but I'm happy to sample the pasta and salad having made it through the morning unscathed, reassuring myself that the afternoon will be more fun as I come to terms with the bike.

After lunch, rested but sweating in my leathers and the

ninety-degree heat, I head out for my third session. Finally, I'm starting to experience something closer to fun than terror. I'm riding, instead of surviving. The tires are scrubbed in and are working well in the heat of early afternoon. I'm finally getting comfortable with the bike and I'm beginning to have the day I'd long anticipated, riding a fun sportbike on a track I've been meaning to sample for years.

"So that's it," you say. "Overconfidence. Probably overcooked a corner and rode it straight into the Mid-Ohio woods, right?"

No, not yet.

By the end of the third session, I'm elated. Not because anyone's going to mistake me for Hodgson or Bostrom, even if my bike does look like theirs. But just because it's finally coming together. I've hit sixth on the back straight and not blown the corner at the end of it. I haven't run off the track by miscalculating the blind turn just past the esses, and I've gotten a knee down in the fast, partially blind and intimidating turn one. The checkered flag is out for the session and I raise my left hand to signal that I'm coming into the pits. The pit entrance at Mid-Ohio is curved and slightly downhill. I'm leaning gently through that curve, left hand still off the grip, already in first gear and already thinking ahead to the next session, when I squeeze some front brake to slow down even more and . . . Wham! I'm on the ground!

Worse yet, I'm lying in the grass with my feet higher than my head and the rear wheel of the Ducati pinning my right leg. I'm splayed out on the ground with all the dignity of a deboned chicken, flopped helplessly in the grass for everyone to see as they ride into the pits, having just locked the front wheel and crashed. In first gear. At maybe 30 mph. On the pit lane entrance.

In the history of motorcycle crashes, many have been worse, but few have been more embarrassing.

A corner worker comes to my rescue and after a minute, I'm able to ride the bike to the garage. The good news is that the damage is limited to brake levers and bodywork. The bad news is that the bodywork is the one thing that makes this bike special. Jason is already on his cell phone ordering replacement parts. Naturally, Ducati wants to display this bike in a few days' time at the AMA Superbike race here at Mid-Ohio. While Jason's on the phone, I'm rehearsing apologies, watching my knee swell, and hoping that other rider still thinks I work for *Cycle World*. I'm hoping he gets my name wrong, too.

It's all history now. I made my apologies, many times over, to the Ducati guys, who were great about the whole thing. I went on to re-injure my knee twice in the following week and eventually endured surgery and physical therapy, just to pay more penance for my stupidity. And I came to terms with the tag I now must forever wear.

Hear about the guy who dropped the only 999s Team USA replica in the country? Crashed it on pit lane! No, really.

I'm that guy.

Having dealt with the stages of anger, denial, grief and whatever else it is they say you go through after an embarrassing crash, there's only one thing left to do. Learn something from it. I relearned two lessons, actually, that apparently weren't ingrained deeply enough.

First, high-performance bikes demand high-performance riding. The powerful brakes that were such a great thing on the Mid-Ohio back straight were still just as powerful when I clumsily squeezed them on pit lane when my mind was somewhere else. Second, there's never an okay time to drop your concentration. Rolling into pit lane, I was already thinking about the next session on the track when I reached for the brake on an unfamiliar bike while in a turn. From there, the inevitability of gravity took over. Shut off your brain, even for a few seconds and you could end up doing something stupid, like dropping the only Team USA 999s in the country. Although at least you don't have to worry about being "that guy."

I'm already him.

CALIFORNIA DREAMING

*California is the center of the motorcycle
industry and culture in the United States, and
the central Pacific Coast Highway is the state's
most famous and stunning jewel.*

If you want to do business with the motorcycle industry in the
United States, you have to go through California, which is not a
bad thing. You know the old saying: It's a nice place to visit, but
I wouldn't want to live there.

California is great for visiting. As a non-resident, you don't have to ride the state's property value roller coaster or worry about the effect of the government's deteriorating bond rating on your tax rates or your kid's school. And, it is indisputably the center of the motorcycle industry in the United States. The Japanese manufacturers have their U.S. headquarters there, and the others, from Harley-Davidson to BMW, at least have a presence in Southern California. Ducati North America used to be based in New Jersey, like BMW, but shifted its base to the west coast a few years back, though it still kept its distance by taking office space in northern California. So even though I've never lived there, because of the industry's clustering in that state, I have found myself visiting often over the years, riding a bizarre-looking Yamaha Morphous scooter along the Huntington Beach waterfront, a BMW R1150GS Adventure on the Angeles Crest Highway (not the perfect match of machine and road, but entertaining, still), a Kawasaki Concours 14 in Sonoma wine country, a Buell Ulysses on the dirt roads of Antelope Valley, a Yamaha R1 on the coils of Mount Palomar and a Ducati Multistrada on the most numbing stretches of Interstate 5 (when I just had to get to Oregon). Even Harley-Davidson, which builds all its motorcycles in the eastern half of the country, maintains a fleet of loaner bikes in southern California. And it's not just for use by the motorcycle press, either. If some suddenly famous TV star with a big Twitter following decides at the last minute he wants to be seen at the huge Love Ride fundraiser on a new Harley, he doesn't have to buy one. His manager calls the Motor Company and one of the press fleet bikes is delivered for his use. It's a good deal if you can get it.

Beyond the manufacturers, a huge portion of the aftermarket industry is based there, in part to be close to the manufacturers.

And more motorcycle publications are based in California than anywhere else, from the big print glossies, such as *Cycle World*, *Motorcyclist* and *Rider*, down to homegrown blogs.

It's the kind of place that nurtures motorcycling obsession. Excellent case in point is Tim Mayhew, a Midwestern guy who moved to California and rode obsessively, wearing out several motorcycles, taking lots of photos along the way and becoming perhaps California's pre-eminent roads scholar. Over the years, he dumped that knowledge into a website (pashnit.com) that started as nothing more than a project for a night class he was taking. Today, that site has grown into a community that attracts tens of thousands of visitors daily. He also operates guided tours and his internet storefront sells motorcycle goods. Passionate, indeed.

California is so large and varied, it could be several states, and several states of mind. I have an odd interest in weather statistics and I often look at the daily numbers for the highest and lowest temperatures in the contiguous forty-eight states. During certain seasons of the year, both the high and the low for the same day are often recorded there. There is little in common between the soaring silence of the Redwood National Forest and the glitz of Hollywood, the concentration of Porsches and Mercedes in La Jolla and the huts of farm workers in the Central Valley, except that they're all in the Golden State. Traveling up Route 5 on that Multistrada, I pulled off at an exit in the Central Valley at sunset and couldn't shake the over-whelming feeling that I was in Texas. The wind, the low-slung Mexican restaurant, the way the dust colored the sky in the sharp angle of the dimming light, and even the smell (a pun-gent mix of truck-stop fumes, diesel, tilled farmland, and livestock) all placed me somewhere west of Dallas, not north of Los Angeles.

Of course any place as large and diverse as California, with 850 miles of coastline, multiple mountain ranges, rainy forests, parched deserts, and opulent vineyards, all scattered over nearly ten degrees of latitude, is certain to offer some incredible destinations to ride to. But the most famous, the most visually spectacular, the most likely to make the motorcycling bucket list is the heart of the Pacific Coast Highway.

The PCH, a.k.a. Highway 1, is more than 600 miles long, and the jewel in the crown is the stretch of about 120 miles between Monterey and Morro Bay. Monterey has its own charms, from its aquarium to the old Cannery Row made famous by John Steinbeck's novel of the same name. The place is hopping when the MotoGP circus is in town at nearby Laguna Seca. It's far more subdued, but rich in eye candy, if cars are your thing, when the Monterey Historic Automobile Races are going on. You may find a car you recognize from the movies, a retired race car with a full pedigree, and someone's personal Lamborghini all parked nonchalantly together around the Monterey Conference Center.

I prefer to do most of my looking from the seat of a moving motorcycle, so I head south on PCH, thumb my nose at the Pebble Beach crowd, which doesn't allow motorcycles on their private road, and as soon as I've slipped past Carmel-by-the-Sea, I've left all that behind. Out here, there's little that's manmade except the road itself, which clings precariously to the coast, climbing and descending the slopes and bluffs where the land ends. There aren't many places to stray from the highway, but if you find the right little dirt roads and trails, such as around Garrapata State Park (*"garrapata"* means "tick" in

Spanish—for the purposes of encouraging tourism, lots of names in the Southwest are better left untranslated), you can slip away from what traffic there is, even in the heavily traveled summer months when RVs are the scourge of the road.

Soon, I come to the Bixby Creek Bridge, and like virtually everyone else who ever came this way, I stop to take a photo. Although built during the Depression, when creating jobs outweighed other concerns, the bridge still demonstrates notable harmony with its spectacular surroundings. With the afternoon sun falling toward the Pacific, its gracefully arched lines glow a soft yellowish-white. Beyond its aesthetic appeal, the Bixby Creek Bridge opened the rugged beauty of Big Sur to automobile traffic, making the little community accessible. John Steinbeck's novels put Monterey on the map, but this dramatic yet quiet coast has a long history of luring writers. Henry Miller lived here for twenty years and the library that bears his name, really a memorial, remains one of Big Sur's few landmarks. Miller testified to the allure of the place. "It may indeed be the highest wisdom to elect to be a nobody in a relative paradise such as this rather than a celebrity in a world which has lost all sense of values," he said. Robert Louis Stevenson (who is credited with coining the often-used phrase "the most felicitous meeting of land and sea" when describing Carmel Bay), Jack London, and Jack Kerouac were among the writers who sought out Big Sur for inspiration, recreation, or even supposed rehabilitation. Kerouac came to this outpost to dry out from his alcoholism and predictably failed. Another famous twentieth-century writer and substance abuser who followed, Hunter S. Thompson, didn't even try.

Today, people come to Big Sur to get married at the Ventana Inn resort, or for lunch at Nepenthe. (When you have an incomparable view of the Pacific from 800 feet above, you can charge $14 for a hamburger and nobody complains.) A little farther south, visitors attend workshops to expand their minds and soak in hot springs at the Esalen Institute. As you see, everybody's doing their own thing out here on the edge of the continent, and so am I.

The PCH clings to the folds of the hills and each time the road dips into an ancient gully cut by eons of erosion, that means another hairpin turn. There can hardly be a sustained stretch of straight road on this voluptuous coast. This is a road you really, really want to see on a motorcycle, both to enjoy the curves rather than dread them in the latter stages of carsickness, and to have the thrust available to pass the RVs or slow-moving sightseers that speckle the landscape. Even in summer, however, when they tend to get thick, they're not really a problem, because every few miles you reach another turnout, another scenic overlook, and Ma and Pa Motorhome are likely to pull over and take in the view. If they don't, you may well want to yourself.

The jewel of PCH is not a road to be treated like a racetrack. A full day to travel this 120-mile length seems just barely enough time. Double back and ride some of the best curves again. Stop at every overlook. Take photos. If the season is right, scan the ocean for the spouts of migrating gray whales, heading north with their newborns. Ride up the goat trail called Nacimiento-Fergusson Road—one of the few places you can turn off between Carmel and Morro Bay and actually escape the coast, if for some insane reason you'd want to—take in more views of the Pacific and then return to the PCH. Hike into the deep shade of the redwoods at Pfeiffer Big Sur State Park. Add more time to your trip if you want to tour the Hearst

Castle at San Simeon and see what could be built with fabulous wealth of the past. Or stop at the Piedras Blancas elephant seal rookery, where thousands of the giant beach slugs bellow, bray, slumber and nuzzle their young in a teeming display. All of this concentrated in one section of coastline as beautiful as you'll find on this earth, and all of it strung along a road that would be a worthy motorcycle destination even if its views were merely ordinary.

After seeing all that the PCH offers, I land at Morro Bay, the seaside town I've somewhat arbitrarily chosen as the southern terminal on my favored stretch of coast. Unlike the natural glory behind me, Morro Bay feels simultaneously homey and hokey to this easterner. T-shirt shops and taffy stands, fishing boats and rental kayaks, waterfront hotels and aged smoke-stacks. A tourist town that still has to work for a living, it's kind of like the Jersey shore, but with nicer landscaping. And, of course, the big rock that everyone (me included) takes a pic-ture of within fifteen minutes of arriving. Sitting by the docks, I listen to the sounds of life on the waterfront: screaming gulls begging for a handout from the fishing boats, sea lions braying hoarsely. As the sun sets over the Pacific and things quiet down, the last sound I hear, and the one I remember most, is the light clicking that rolls in from the bay. In the fading light I spot the source. An otter dives, brings up a clam, sets it on his chest as he floats in the still water, then cracks it open with a rock to enjoy his dinner. Click! Click! It lingers in my memory as the quaint punctuation to my mental slide show of memora-ble PCH images, a peaceful, end-of-day sound that must seem charming to everyone except the clams.

From the famed motorcycle roads up Mount Palomar and along the Angeles Crest, to the popular motorcycle hangouts such as the Rock Store and Alice's Restaurant, California offers lots of reasons to make motorcyclists pashnit. It's an obvious, even clichéd choice, but if I have only one California ride left, I want it to start where the MotoGP bikes roar, end where the otters click, and leave enough free time in between to be a nobody right where Henry Miller admired a westward-looking country's last, best view. It's a great place to visit.

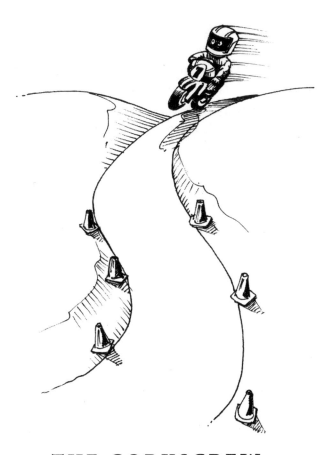

THE CORKSCREW

What does it feel like to ride off the side of a building? The closest most of us can hope to come is experiencing Laguna Seca's signature turn, the Corkscrew.

Riding uphill on the Rahal Straight at Mazda Raceway Laguna Seca, the world appears two-dimensional, reduced to blocks of vibrant colors glowing in the sun like a bright abstract painting. Below the horizon, from left to right, there's first a light dusty brown, the color of northern California soil that can't remember the feel of rain. Then, a strip of bright blue-and-white curbing. Next, directly ahead, is the broad swath of black asphalt that is the track, another thin stripe of blue and white, and then more brown.

That's below the straight unforgiving line of the horizon. Above the horizon is vast, unbroken blue, just a shade darker than the curbs, and it's that stark expanse that's so intimidating. No trees, no buildings, no reference points. Just blue sky, like I'm about to ride into orbit.

I'm sure there's more than that, beyond my peripheral vision on both sides, but I really don't have time to look right now. Just brown, white, black and blue. My world, for that second, is reduced to four colors, a dose of trepidation, a tingle of anticipation, and a heap of intense concentration. It's the concentration that matters most, because what looks like a two-dimensional abstract painting is really the approach to the best-known and most unique signature curve in U.S. roadracing, and what is actually the most three-dimensional slice of race track you're likely to find anywhere. If I get it wrong, I'll become a dust plume in that dry California dirt, and that's the memory I least want to take home.

Welcome to the Corkscrew. Of all the named and famed curves on all the storied racetracks in the United States, Laguna Seca's Corkscrew would be the last one I'd want to miss out on before I shuffle out of this motorcycle-riding life. So when the opportunity to test ride a Buell 1125R at Laguna fell into my lap just days before my birthday, it felt like an early present.

The black asphalt draped over these brown California hills outside Monterey has a certain weight of history and a stiff reputation that many tracks in this country lack. History has been written here by fast vehicles with two and four wheels: Grand Prix motorcycles in the two-stroke era and MotoGP bikes every Fourth of July (or thereabouts) in recent years; Superbikes, both at the world and national levels; Indy Cars in the CART days and sports car prototypes today; the annual Monterey Historic Automobile Races, which bring collectible cars and a country club atmosphere to the track's blind turns and steep elevation changes. And the most famous of all of Laguna's corners is the Corkscrew, a ninety-degree left at the very highest point on the entire track that plunges over what appears to be the side of a cliff and then instantly swerves back to the right as the track swoops downhill to the next challenge. For the bravest and canniest racers, Laguna's most famous turn is a passing opportunity. For everyone, it's an opportunity for disaster.

It's also like no other corner in U.S. roadracing. MotoGP and AMA Superbike champ Nicky Hayden has called the Corkscrew "the best corner in the world" and fellow MotoGP racer and former World Superbike Champion Colin Edwards once claimed that "Once you understand the physics involved, it's pretty easy." (Of course Edwards also added that if you get too aggressive about it, "it could be all asses and elbows in no time.") Among car racing fans, possibly the most famous Corkscrew moment was when the uncannily talented Alex Zanardi just dispensed with the turn altogether and went straight through the California dirt, somehow not destroying his Indy Car, somehow not suffering a penalty from the race stewards for cutting the course, and somehow avoiding a collision as he lurched back on the track, to steal what appeared to be Bryan

Herta's first-ever Indy Car victory with his (choose your adjective) inspired, unintentional, spectacularly lucky, blatantly illegal, or horribly irresponsible last-lap pass.

Before we rode the track on the Buell 1125R, we talked with former racer and company founder Erik Buell, who told stories of his own about racing against Kenny Roberts in the 1970s on an ill-mannered but powerful two-stroke Yamaha TZ750 at Laguna Seca. Any story about Laguna Seca eventually involves the Corkscrew. "It was great fun on a TZ750," Buell said. "You'd just lift the front and turn it on the back wheel like a motocrosser."

Maybe great fun for you, Erik. I can't even "lift the front and turn it on the back wheel" if I *am* riding a motocrosser, so forget about imitating that act on a four-cylinder two-stroke with a legendary reputation for tossing riders off its back like an enraged rodeo bull. Fortunately, before our first riding session we also get some highly practical advice from former MotoGP racer Jeremy McWilliams, who raced a Buell XBRR in the Daytona 200 a few years ago and is on hand to brief us before our first session on the track. His advice for the Corkscrew is simple, stark and to be ignored at your own personal peril: Keep right, hugging the right side of the track as you top the rise. You'll see an orange cone set by the right curb, just off the track. Don't initiate your turn to the left until your front wheel is even with that cone, McWilliams warns us. "You'll want to start your turn sooner," he said. "But don't."

Having read and heard about so many racers' experiences with Laguna, it's finally my turn to see the track at my much slower pace. We roll out for a few recon laps behind Buell press guy Paul James, the 1125R's V-twin rumbling beneath me, a few butterflies rumbling deep within me. Then we're turned loose to run our own pace, and I finally get to experience the Corkscrew for myself.

Here's what it feels like to me.

Back to the Rahal Straight, which creates that sensation of looking at a five-colored wall that I mentioned above. Brown, blue, white: all colors I want to avoid. Black, the color of asphalt and tires, is the one I want to stay on. Doing strictly as told by McWilliams, I hug the right edge of the black asphalt as I rise over the crest at the end of the Rahal Straight, braking as I reach the plateau and make one final downshift. If I thought that now, at the highest point on the track, I'd be able to see everything ahead, I'd be mistaken. The Corkscrew isn't letting me off that easy. All I can see is that the track makes a ninety-degree left and drops off into parts unseen.

Of all my bad riding habits, turning in early is one I constantly battle. You'll never find a pro racer or a riding instructor who extols the virtues of an early apex, but anxiety gnaws at my patience and whispers in my ear, "turn now, turn now." But with McWilliams' advice stuck in my mind like the word of God (only with an Irish accent), I check my worst impulses and force myself to wait until my front wheel comes even with that orange cone before banking left. Then, I plunge over the edge, like riding off the side of a building. It was with this very moment in mind that I showed restraint at the morning breakfast buffet. My guts rise to press against my lungs, the bike feels light, and any feelings of two-dimensional illusions are vaporized. As I fall over the edge and finally get to see the track ahead of me, the importance of following McWilliams' advice is instantly obvious in a way that sears the information into my mind for all future laps. If I had aimed the bike in the direction I would expect the track to go, if I had started my turn early and lined up for a sweeping curve like I'd expect to find on any other track, I'd be six feet into the gravel and dirt. Instead, thanks to my strict adherence to McWilliams' recommended line, I'm still on the black as gravity sucks me downward a few stories while I shift from left lean to right lean. The racers say the fast way through the Corkscrew is to keep right after making the plunge and to hold the throttle wide open while gaining velocity down the hill into Rainey Curve. Personally, I'm looking for the survival line, not the fast line, but they seem to be about the same. And be assured, my throttle is nowhere near wide open.

Make no mistake about all this—there's no bravado, no bragging in this account. I'm riding at parade-lap speeds for the MotoGP riders who come here once a year. Not for the first time, I'm forced to consider the huge gulf between the skills of us ordinary riders and those of the true pros. I'm just trying not to wad a borrowed Buell, make a fool of myself, or sample the local medical facilities. The real racers charge into that intimidating turn at double my speed, tires slewing and clawing for traction at the extreme edge of rubber's ability to grip asphalt, while fighting for position with twenty aggressive competitors, all inches apart, all under the influence of surging adrenaline, an inhuman level of competitiveness, and intense pressure to win.

That skill differential between those of us who sit on the sofa and watch the television and those on center stage is just as big in all sports, whether the challenge is trying to sprint 100 meters in a shade over nine seconds at the Olympics or nail a three-pointer in the NBA Finals while a six-foot-ten power forward with a massive wingspan charges toward your face. It just happens that what I do is ride a motorcycle. I'll never stand on an Olympic podium or know what it feels like to match Nicky Hayden's pace around a track. But, when I'm old and infirm and have to hang up the leathers, at least I'll have memories of what it feels like, more or less, to ride off the side of a building. I'll always have memories of the Corkscrew.

EVOLUTION ISLAND

*Welcome to the unique motorcycling culture of
Puerto Rico, where the motorcycle cops ride
cruisers, messengers rule the urban streets,
and the riding's great 365 days a year (except
for hurricanes).*

As even semi-attentive junior high school students know,
Charles Darwin's theory of evolution owes much to his observations of the Galapagos Islands. Isolated from the influences
of the larger world by miles of open water, forms of life on the
Galapagos developed in ways unseen elsewhere. When I first
moved to the island of Puerto Rico, I found a similar situation
in the local motorcycle culture.

It was the early 1990s, and some motorcycle trends in the United States that are now mostly played out were back then just picking up momentum. The Harley-Davidson boom years were beginning, fueled in part by middle-aged Baby Boomers in their peak spending years, many of them re-entry riders. Meanwhile, for the Japanese companies, sportbikes were becoming more important and the classes were growing more standardized, which would lead to intense competition to build the sharpest, fastest, and most competitive 600cc and 1000cc racer replicas. The U.S. motorcycle market grew more polarized, with many riders wanting either a street-legal race bike or a Big Twin Harley, and when the latter became too common, we were treated to the unexpected phenomenon of $50,000 customs that were barely rideable and semi-articulate bike builders starring in their own television shows.

I landed in Puerto Rico as those trends were just getting started and found that the island had a motorcycling vibe and culture all its own. Remember the mid-1990s Honda Nighthawk 750? Probably not. In a way, the Nighthawk did make a kind of sense on paper. It was intended to attract those re-entry riders with its low price, minimal maintenance and an engine designed to be familiar to Boomers, an air-cooled 750cc four. But it never caught on because it flew directly into the teeth of the prevailing trends. It lacked the high-tech features, serious performance and the full-coverage bodywork sought by sportbike buyers and its nondescript styling was a throwback to the 1970s Universal Japanese Motorcycle, not a modern riff on the nostalgia for 1950s American styling that was driving Harley sales. You rarely saw a Nighthawk on the road in the United States. In San Juan, however, they were the most common motorcycles on the streets, at least Monday through Friday, but not for any reason Honda had ever imagined. Instead, it was because they were the choice of San Juan's messenger fleet—cheap to buy, easy to maintain, powerful enough for urban work and durable enough to stand up to long days of lane-splitting through gridlock in tropical heat. In Puerto Rico, I saw plenty of Nighthawks with the identifying cube-shaped metal box bolted to the rear for carrying documents or other deliveries, painful-looking dents in the tank and cracked turn signal stalks sagging like the fractured antenna of some wounded insect, but still running strong after 80,000 hard urban miles.

The messengers themselves were a unique motorcycle subculture. They clustered in front of the major banks and office buildings in the Hato Rey sector of San Juan, waiting for the radio to crackle with an assignment. When the delivery order came, they roared off through traffic, every acceleration full throttle. Splitting lanes was the norm; when that failed, cutting down a sidewalk was not uncommon. Sometimes the rider left his helmet perched on top of his head, so he was looking out beneath the chin bar, the better to smoke a cigarette while riding through traffic. I'm surprised to report that the messengers haven't totally been eliminated by e-mail, though their numbers are visibly diminished. Today, they get their orders over cell phones, instead of radios, but they still tend to ride battered and grimy old Nighthawks with bravado.

Here's another forgotten nugget of unimportant moto-trivia I wouldn't remember except for how Puerto Rico turned some stereotypes inside out. In those days, there was an ad that appeared in some of the motorcycle magazines, I think by Kawasaki, that tried to play off the bad-ass image some cruiser riders like to project. The ad depicted the new machine, with the unfettered wanderer of motorcycle mythology aboard and riding into town, and the local sheriff telling himself, "I'll have to keep an eye on that one."

In Puerto Rico, that stereotype fell apart. The so-called "bad guys" weren't riding cruisers. The police were. The police fleet consisted of a motley mix of Honda Shadows, Yamaha Viragos, and even Suzuki Intruders. The Intruders, particularly, were bikes built for style first, with function a distant afterthought (and functionality for law enforcement not even thought of at all by the designers, I'm sure). Any truly dangerous characters who were on motorcycles were far more likely to be riding sportbikes than cruisers. The U.S. magazines running the Kawasaki ad made their way to the island, but the pitch didn't translate.

I evolved in Puerto Rico, too. Some people who met me later in life were surprised to learn I had owned a Harley-Davidson Sportster, a motorcycle I'd be unlikely to buy now that I live in the Midwestern United States. But in San Juan, where lane-splitting was a daily requirement, the bike's narrowness and low-end grunt more than made up for the lack of sheer speed. Nowhere on the island was there a road with a speed limit higher than 55 mph, and although my Sportster was among the first to be graced with a five-speed transmission, the narrow backroads in the island's central mountains are so tightly snarled that one day I realized I had ridden 100 miles without ever shifting into fifth.

For me, Puerto Rico was a motorcycling dream. Good riding weather 365 days a year (barring hurricanes), endless strings of mountain roads that seemed to be mostly a series of second-gear curves connecting short straights that offered views of deep canyons and trickling waterfalls. I rode to humble but excellent restaurants hidden in the tightly tucked folds of those lush mountains and to beaches where the water shifted among dozens of shades of blue and green. And all of this suffused with a friendly, life-loving, 500-year-old culture that mixed Spanish, Latin American and U.S. influences into a new and tangy *salsa* not quite like anywhere else.

Given all the advantages of riding a motorcycle, I was amazed that more people didn't. The reasons are several, but I believe the main one has to do with that unique mix that is the Puerto Rican culture. The island was a Spanish colony for a little over 400 years before becoming a U.S. colony in 1898, which happens to be just before motor vehicles sputtered onto the scene. Thus, Puerto Rico's relationship with the road more resembles that of the United States (cars are the real deal, motorcycles are "toys") than that of Spain (where kids start out riding a scooter, not driving a car, and motorcycle racing is among the most popular sports).

Swimming against the tide of both U.S. and Puerto Rican car-centered culture, I decided that living just over eighteen degrees north of the equator meant I didn't need a car at all, so I adopted a car-free, carefree way of life. I did the grocery shopping a little more frequently than I'd like and I always kept a rainsuit handy for the tropical showers that could unleash themselves at any moment. I learned, the hard way, that when one of your co-workers unexpectedly gives you a fresh coconut from his backyard tree, it's really hard to transport it home with nothing more than a bungee net (nope, didn't make it). I considered none of those issues to be inconveniences, much less problems, and after almost two years, I married an island woman who, of course, had her own car, and then there was even less need for me to think about buying one. So I never did.

The positives of riding were magnified by all the daily annoyances I avoided by not driving a car. Lane-splitting through San Juan traffic meant that a rush-hour trip across town on the Sportster might take a third as long as the same trip in a car. For a while, I lived in the historic district of Old San Juan, with its narrow streets that were laid out centuries ago when a few horses constituted heavy traffic. Every car in Old San Juan had dents on at least one corner from the nightly parallel parking battles and my neighbors complained incessantly about parking woes. Their choices were to rent an expensive spot in one of the three parking garages or hope to find an open spot on the street. And if they came home late on a Friday or Saturday, when the Old City bars were packed, all hope was lost. Meanwhile, I convinced the owner of the apartment building where I lived to allow me to roll my motorcycle into the small interior courtyard of the building. I was probably the only person in Old San Juan to have free, indoor, off-street parking.

Over the eight years I lived on the island, I explored all 78 municipalities, 76 of them by motorcycle (two require a boat or plane). I enjoyed a Christmas Toy Run without fear of freezing, checked out the local racing scene, and joined a group ride or two. But there was still more of the motorcycling culture for me to experience when I decided to import a bike from the mainland United States.

In 1998, having worked for three months on a very intense but temporary job that involved demanding daily deadlines, I found myself with a unexpected chunk of change in the bank and a desire to reward myself for all those mornings I was up at 6:30 to get my work done by noon. At the time, the Sportster was the only motorcycle in the garage and I was feeling an urge to ride something with a little more performance. Sticker shock set in the moment I entered a motorcycle showroom, however, and looking at used bikes in the classifieds was only slightly better. In my view, a lack of competition was to blame for the inflated prices on an island with a per capita income lower than any of the fifty states. Each manufacturer basically viewed all of Puerto Rico, despite its 4 million residents, as one market and established one distributor that functioned as a dealer. Independent dealers usually didn't last long or prosper, because they had to get their new motorcycles through the one approved distributor/dealer. It was hard to compete when you were totally dependent for product on your biggest, strongest competitor. Another contributor to the high price tags was the import tax. At that time, there was no sales tax in Puerto Rico, but all incoming goods were taxed at import.

On the other hand, shipping a motorcycle by boat from Florida to Puerto Rico only cost about $300, and I quickly calculated that I could pay for an airline ticket to Florida, buy a nearly new, used bike that would not be taxed as heavily as a new one, and still come out well ahead. And, I could choose from some motorcycles that would be difficult or impossible to find on the island. Scanning the online ads, I identified two likely prospects and took off for Florida. Within a few days, I'd bought a Triumph Speed Triple and booked it a cruise on a cargo ship sailing from Jacksonville for San Juan. With no Triumph dealer in Puerto Rico, I figured I'd have the only Speed Triple on the island.

Of course the motorcycle dealership salesmen had tried to scare me with warnings about the endless, expensive process of getting an imported bike through the Puerto Rico tax and motor vehicles bureaucracies. But I fortified myself with advice from experienced hands, carefully collected paperwork from the shipping company, stood in the appropriate lines at the import offices, paid my fees and after a long day of standing and waiting was finally authorized to rescue my Triumph from the weed-studded, fenced-in parking lot at the port where it had sat for a couple of days. With my documents in order and the bike in my possession, all that was left was to get my Puerto Rico title and registration. The clerk went through my pile of paperwork and receipts, and just as I was smugly thinking I'd conquered the bureaucracy, he asked me a question I'd never imagined: Where's the proof that the motorcycle has been washed?

Excuse me?

The U.S. Department of Agriculture requires that all imported vehicles have to be washed, he explained, to prevent unintentional importation of things like, in my case, strange Florida insects.

Standing there with my tax receipts, shipping documents, and meticulously compiled paperwork, I could only try to appreciate the irony—I had survived the San Juan bureaucracy, just to be shot down by an unexpected lightning bolt emanating from Washington.

The situation was absurd in the extreme. If some pair of amorous and environmentally hazardous Florida beetles had squirreled themselves away behind the instrument pod of my Triumph, intent on a honeymoon in Puerto Rico, they had already had two days to hop off my bike and flee into a nearby weedy field to begin propagating their own kind and wreaking havoc on the ecosystem. A little soap and water would be a bit late, but I knew there was no point arguing logic in the face of a legal requirement of the federal bureaucracy. And although I knew the answer, I still had to ask the question. Could I wash it myself? No, he replied predictably. The feds had to have their piece of paper.

I rode the Triumph to a nearby gas station and car wash and tried to explain my dilemma to the attendant. He was incredulous at first, thinking that I wanted to ride my motorcycle through his automated car wash. No, I laboriously explained, what I wanted was one of his car wash *receipts*, and I was perfectly willing to pay the full price of a car wash to get one. Once we reached an understanding, I got my receipt, he sprayed the motorcycle with a hose to satisfy at least a few letters of the law (and leave water-spot evidence, in the unlikely event the bureaucrat checked for actual washing), and I went back to the motor vehicles office, got my title, registration and license plate, and rode off happily on what I presumed to be the only Triumph Speed Triple in Puerto Rico. Which clearly was, as Darwin could have told you, not a species native to the uniquely evolved ecosystem of that island.

TOLLS
Buggy: 15 cents
Horse & Rider: 6 cents
Sheep or Pigs: 2 cents
Person Going to Church: Free

RIDING THE
BOURBON TRAIL

*On a Kentucky country lane, I smell scents
from my childhood: hay drying in the sun, the
damp fecundity of a trickling creek. Then one
not from my youth. Whiskey? Out here?*

Smells are registered deep in the animal part of our brains, which is why they trigger such visceral reactions and drag to the surface unexpectedly strong memories we thought were forever lost to the hazy past. Riding along McCracken Pike, a narrow little traffic-free Kentucky country lane that assures me it's leading to absolutely nothing, the smells are pinging my synapses, dredging up scraps of my childhood. The freshly cut hay in the small roadside fields is the strongest of these, taking me back to boyhood days working in the summer sun on my grandfather's farm, putting up hay for the winter. I catch a hint of the coppery tang of a natural gas well, and the early-summer odors of woodland fecundity as I pass a shallow creek, where water trickles over brown stones, just like the creek and woods I scouted as a boy in West Virginia.

Then an odor wafts into my helmet that has nothing to do with my childhood, a smell so seemingly out of place on this rural lane that I'm sure I must be mistaken. Whiskey? Out here?

Then I round a corner and see the stately buildings of the Woodford Reserve distillery, where people have been making whiskey with few interruptions since Elijah Pepper, one of the earliest distillers in the Bluegrass region, set up operations here alongside Glenn's Creek in 1812.

Ah, yes, the Bourbon Trail. These are not the finest roads for motorcycle riding, if you're looking for the most snarled hairpins, the most precipitous mountain slopes or high-speed ridge-top sweepers. No, the roads of the Bourbon Trail are a lot like the product the region is known for. They offer an unpretentious yet high-quality charm, are best enjoyed without an excess of hurry, and always command a certain level of respect and responsibility. The road past Woodford Reserve is a fitting example. The pavement is narrow and sight lines are often interrupted by abrupt curves. Lush summer foliage grows right up to where the white lines would be (if there were any). This is no place to charge ahead heedlessly. No one says you can't enjoy an adult pace, but this road is best savored respectfully, like sipping a glass of bourbon thoughtfully, appreciatively, instead of downing it in a shot and slamming the glass down on the bar for another.

Entering the Bourbon Trail area from the east, the roads around Frankfort offer views of the expansive (and expensive) horse farms with endless white fences and soaring barns topped with copper cupolas. Thoroughbreds worth more than my house graze in pastures more lush and neatly trimmed than my front lawn. Kentucky is a state of church-going people with an economy built on old-fashioned sins: smoking, gambling and drinking; tobacco, race horses and bourbon. Personally, I'm in no doubt about which of the three is most interesting. I don't smoke or chew tobacco, and the smallest amount of horse racing is usually enough to satisfy my interest and relieve me of my stake. Bourbon, however, is my favorite alcoholic beverage, and even if you don't favor that form of whiskey, seeing how it's made is an interesting afternoon's education and getting to the distilleries along the Bourbon Trail provides an above-average day's ride.

I ride west out of the town of Versailles (Kentucky pronunciation: ver-SALES) on U.S. 62 and just a few miles short of the town of Lawrenceburg the road descends a wooded slope above the Kentucky River, makes a hard turn onto an old concrete bridge, and rising before me is the huge Austin Nichols distillery, best known for making Wild Turkey. With the practiced readiness of people who believe in a slogan, the folks at Austin Nichols like to say that they'd rather make their whiskey fancy than make their buildings fancy. Indeed, while all the distilleries have at least one welcoming building that feels like an old southern mansion, only newer, the majority of this huge distillery definitely projects an industrial ambiance. Everything is huge. The fermentation vats hold 30,000 gallons and the still is forty feet tall. The warehouses where the whiskey is aged hold 20,000 barrels.

I've already begun my education on the art of bourbon making with some advance reading, but the tour fills in the particulars. The name comes from Bourbon County, Kentucky. In the early 1800s, whiskey made there was stored in huge barrels with "Bourbon" stamped on the side as the site of origin. They were shipped south to New Orleans on flatboats where the Kentucky whiskey's reputation was forever sealed. Today, bourbon isn't made in Bourbon County, but the name is carefully guarded. By law, at least 51 percent of the grain in bourbon must be corn. To that, the distillers add varying proportions of rye, malted barley, yeast, and a bit of the leftover grain mix from a previous batch, the "sour mash" that both gives this type of whiskey its name and also assures more consistent results. The mixture of those ingredients is allowed to ferment and is distilled. The result is a clear liquid, called "white dog," that is high in alcohol but lacking the color and flavor of bourbon. That flavor comes from the aging process, which is also regulated by law. Oak barrels are charred inside by a gas-fired flame. The distilled liquor is placed in these barrels for aging and, through winter and summer, heat and cold, it expands and contracts, seeping into the charred oak and taking on the flavor and color that makes it bourbon. After the years of aging, the barrels are never as full when opened as they were when they were first put into the warehouses, as some small amount evaporates through the barrel. The portion that escapes is called the "angels' share," and that's what my nose detected when I was still half a mile from the Woodford Reserve distillery on McCracken Pike.

Tour any of the distilleries and you will see the barrels

stacked floor to ceiling, waiting for years before the bourbon is ready to be bottled and sold. By law, Kentucky bourbon must be aged at least two years. If it has been aged less than four years, that must be noted on the bottle. Many brands are aged seven to eight years or longer. Also by law, the oak barrels can only be used once to make bourbon. Some of the old ones are sold around the world for making other liquors, from sherry to scotch. Some are sawed in half and end up in the front yards of local residents, where they are used as large flower pots. You'll see them overflowing with petunias or pansies as you ride past.

Leaving behind the birthplace of Wild Turkey, I ramble west along U.S. 62 through tiny towns and stands of woods into Bardstown, where My Old Kentucky Home State Park celebrates the past. Tour guides in nineteenth-century costumes show off the mansion made famous in Stephen Collins Foster's song. If you want to learn more about bourbon's past, wander over to the Oscar Getz Museum of Whiskey History. First of all, though, lunch is calling. I wedge the rear tire against a downtown curb and walk into an old-style lunch counter of the type that can still be found in small towns across the country, if you're lucky and if you avoid the monotonous, chain-store strip that's been regurgitated in nearly identical form on the outskirts of every town and city in the United States. The dim light inside promises coolness, a sign you learn to look for in the South. Retired men wearing well-aged caps linger over chicken, conversation, and coffee in a corner booth, while local insurance agents and clerks from the county courthouse in shirtsleeves and ties drop in to pick up "to-go" orders from waitresses they know by name. My kind of place, when I'm on the road.

Fortified by lunch, I'm ready to see the smaller-scale side of today's bourbon production, so I ride south on Kentucky

Route 49 in search of the birthplace of my favorite bourbon of them all: Maker's Mark. Not only do the folks at Maker's Mark turn out a good product, but they also put on a great tour. This distillery, which is also a National Historic Landmark, dates to 1805, and its grounds resemble a park with clapboard buildings painted a distinctive charcoal gray with red shutters and the stone-lined Whiskey Creek cutting through its trimmed lawns. Compared to Austin Nichols, the ambience is fancier, yet in a down-home way, if such a thing is possible. Entering the grounds, I pass the old Toll House, where a sign lists the costs of using the road, long before motorcycles were imagined: 15 cents for a buggy, 6 cents for a horse and rider, 2 cents for sheep or pigs, and free for persons going to church. The Maker's Mark folks put as much effort into presentation as they do into making their whiskey.

Of course while tours of the distillery are a nice way to make customers feel more connected, the real focus is the product in the bottle. In Maker's Mark, it's also about what's on the bottle. The most obvious distinctive characteristic of Maker's Mark is the red wax seal on every bottle. After seeing the huge numbers of bottles being sealed mechanically at the huge Austin Nichols distillery, it's an abrupt change of gears to learn that here every bottle is hand-dipped in that bright red wax. If you'd like, you can buy a bottle and dip it yourself. The even more important but less obvious difference between Maker's Mark and other bourbons, however, is in the ingredients. Where the others use rye, the Maker's Mark recipe calls for red winter wheat, which imparts a mellower flavor. And makes it my personal choice.

I won't question your intelligence by telling you about the inherent dangers of mixing motorcycles and liquor. Anyone likely to pick up this book already knows enough about riding to understand the risks. Also, if you're like most of us who ride, you're stubborn and independent enough to respond poorly to lectures. But since I'm the one who mixed motorcycles and alcohol in this story, I will risk going so far as to tell you my personal policy. It's a simple one that some may consider too rigid, but it works for me. When I ride, I don't drink. Not even one beer, not a single glass of bourbon. The reason why? What you lose when you drink that is even more important than reflexes and coordination is your judgment. If I have to decide how much is too much, I'd be doing so after compromising my ability to muster the good judgment needed to make that assessment. On the other hand, if zero is the only acceptable level, absolutely no judgment is required to gauge my sobriety.

I tend to enjoy my favorite experiences undiluted, unadulterated, held in isolation from distractions, as much as possible. I most enjoy riding when I can reduce it to its essential elements, just me and the motorcycle and the road (or a track, which even more effectively focuses the experience), and I prefer to make full use of all my senses, undulled, when riding. The same way I like my coffee black and my bourbon straight, or at most with a little ice if the day's warm.

What I've found is that the more you know about the experiences you enjoy, the more you appreciate and savor them. That's certainly true with riding. Every riding course I've ever taken has not only introduced new skills and sharpened old ones, but has also made me appreciate even more those sublime moments when it all comes together in an enjoyable task well performed. For the same reason, a ride down the Bourbon Trail, and the education that comes from seeing the work, craftsmanship, and care that go into each bottle, makes the bourbon taste even better at the end of the day's ride.

BLIND DATE IN VERMONT

The Motogiro USA vintage road rally
unleashes a flotilla of forty-year-old tiddlers
on New England back roads for a weekend of
quirky competition.

Married 46-year-old male seeks unique dance partner for memorable weekend in Vermont. Italian ancestry a plus, but not essential. Must be at least 38 years old and under 250. In-continent oil-drippers frowned upon, but let's be honest: I can't afford to be picky.

For two months, Bob Coy has been living up to his last name, and I'm as curious as a guy on a blind date when I arrive at the Grey Bonnet Inn near Killington, Vermont for the 2006

Motogiro USA vintage road rally. Coy, one of the event organizers, promised he'd have an eligible bike for me to ride. But he never said which bike, or even what kind. So as I arrive in Vermont, all I know is what I've gleaned about the Motogiro USA from reading the rules: The bike must be no newer than a 1968 model and no larger than 250cc in displacement. Because of those two rules, I can also safely say it will be a motorcycle I have never ridden before. And I'll be expected to ride this borrowed antique across 250 paved and unpaved miles of Vermont back roads over the course of the weekend, reach various checkpoints on schedule, and compete in multiple "ability tests" along the way.

Coy greets me warmly at the registration desk and then hands me off to John Strempfer. Strempfer, who handles schmoozing duties for the United States Classic Racing Association, is exactly the kind of guy you can yak about motorcycles with all day the first time you meet him and it's just like you've known him for years. But of course I steer the conversation to the central question on my mind. "What the heck am I riding, John?"

"A Motobi 125," he says.

I wonder if the blank expression on my face reveals that I've never even heard of a Motobi 125. Hey, I admit, Mr. Vintage Expert Guy I am not.

Strempfer launches into a story about the Benelli brothers having a spat back in the 1950s, with one of the brothers stomping off in a huff to build motorcycles called Motobis. It all sounds very Italian. As for mechanical particulars, he explains that a Motobi 125 is a four-stroke with a single, air-cooled, horizontal cylinder. The five-speed gearbox is operated by a heel-toe shifter on the right side. In reverse pattern.

The rear brake pedal is on the left side. So I'm trying to get my mind around the concept of downshifting by pushing down with the heel of what I've always considered my braking foot when I realize, I really ought to test ride this thing before I'm expected to perform anything called an "ability test," or even mingle with unsuspecting Vermont traffic.

Strempfer has prepped the Motobi in his shop, so we fill it with his proprietary witch's brew of high-octane race gas and it's ready to roll. He runs through the starting drill. Bike on the centerstand (there is no sidestand). Turn on main petcock. Choke on. Tickle the carb. Stand on the left side of the bike and kick the kickstarter with my right foot. Give her a blip of throttle at just the right moment and she fires on the first try.

"Don't be afraid to rev her," Strempfer tells me, with an encouraging slap on the back. "She likes to be revved." Of course there's no tachometer to tell me how many revs the little piston is pulling as I buzz out of the inn's parking lot in the quickly fading light of dusk. A true Italian *piloto* of 1967 would just *know*. As I pull onto Vermont 100 for my quick shakedown run, the tiny headlight barely squeezes a weak glimmer past the really cool-looking old-style number plate affixed to the front of the bike, and the taillight glows dimly behind me when the revs are high, then fades to nearly nothing when the engine is idling. No mirror has yet been fitted to the bike. No turn signals. Nearly invisible in the dusk, clueless to what's behind me, I'm wondering if some inattentive Vermont driver is going to overlook me in the semi-darkness and plaster me and my slow-moving Motobi into vintage Italian road paste.

Here comes the first curve. The bike is so light and narrow that the mere thought of turning is enough to change direction. The old-style ribbed front tire is new and it feels like I can count each transition to one more rib as the bike leans. It also feels like if I lean just one rib too far, I'll lowside right into the Vermont shrubbery. Okay, that's enough. Time for a U-turn. That's when I learn about 1960s Italian drum brakes. I apply the gradual squeeze that works so well with modern disc brakes. The result? Squeeze, nothing, squeeze a little more, still nothing, squeeze a bit harder, near lockup! I turn around and then rev the *pistone* out of the Italian Job to climb the gentle hill back to the inn, barely sustaining 40 mph, praying that no impatient driver will crowd me from behind, that no car will emerge from a side road and force me into a panic braking situation that would surely involve more panic than braking. Then, with relief, I'm back in the hotel parking lot, grinning like a fool. Thrilled just to be back without crashing Bob Coy's collectible Italian motorcycle. I've ridden less than two miles and the Motogiro hasn't even started yet, but it's already been an intense experience. Like the total vintage newbie I am, I'm soon jabbering enthusiastically to Strempfer about the revvy engine, the lightness of the motorcycle, the near dartiness of the handling.

"You know," Strempfer mentions casually, "those tires are brand new and I have a habit of really, really putting a lot of air pressure in the tires to make sure they're seated properly and sometimes I forget to check them later." I go silent. Pulling out my tire gauge, I check the pressure: 56 psi front; 64 psi rear. Well, that would explain the darty handling. I adjust the Motobi's tire pressure to non-explosive levels and wander off to my room, hoping for a good night's sleep before the Motogiro starts in the morning.

If this whole Motogiro concept sounds like a good time— riding vintage motorcycles around great New England back roads with just enough competition thrown in to get the middle-aged juices flowing—then just imagine the original it's based on. The original Motogiro d'Italia is the kind of event that's impossible to imagine happening today, and for young riders, it may be hard to imagine there was ever such a time and place when an all-out race on public roads was one of the biggest things in the motorcycling world. The Motogiro began in 1914 but it peaked in popularity and importance after World War II. In 1954, 50 motorcycle manufacturers (not 50 riders, but 50 *manufacturers*) entered the Motogiro and marques such as Ducati, MV Agusta, Gilera, Benelli, Moto Guzzi and others built motorcycles specifically for the event. The world's best and most famous racers lined up beside ordinary Italian Giuseppes to race their way around Italy, constantly in danger of flying off the edge of an Alpine cliff or smacking into Signore Romano's cow as it ambled across the road. The Motogiro was too cool to live. In 1957, the Italian government put an end to racing on the public roads. But in 2001, the Motogiro d'Italia got a modern reincarnation. Those old bikes were pulled out of retirement to ride the same old roads, but now it was a time trial, not a race. Vintage enthusiasts from all over the world came to pilot aging motorcycles through the Italian countryside, make brilliant roadside repairs and relive a few of the glory days. It was such great fun that some U.S. riders imported the concept, and the Motogiro USA was born.

In the U.S. version riders are sent off in 30-second intervals. As the official starter releases me, I ride north on Vermont 100 in the last fog of morning. Just 4.4 miles later I leave pavement as the route sends us up steep South Hill Road. The Motogiro's Vermont back roads route is dirt as often as it's paved, but the Motobi is so light and the weather conditions so perfect, I buzz along at about the same modest speed, regardless of whether asphalt is beneath my tires or not. My fellow competitors are easy to spot, because we're all wearing numbered white bibs and riding old, slow, sometimes broken-down motorcycles. Locals have been told to expect us, and we get a surprising number of friendly waves on rural roads and in small towns alike. Some folks have set up lawn chairs in their front yards to watch us buzz, brap, and belch past. Occasionally, a "big" 250 comes roaring past my pristine little Motobi, but with similar frequency I pass old Triumphs or Bultacos or whatnot stopped along the road, a rider poking at the machine's guts in hopes of getting fire in the hole again.

The competition aspect of the Motogiro consists of two parts: First, keep your bike running and navigate the course to reach specified checkpoints on schedule. All you have to do to meet the schedule is maintain an average speed of around 25 mph. The second, more difficult part consists of the ability tests. The first of these takes place right next to the village green in the little town of Bristol. The test course consists of eight cones and the goal is to weave through them in exactly 16.5 seconds without putting a foot down or knocking over cones. Penalties are added for dabbing a foot or tipping a cone and for the amount of deviation from the goal time of 16.5 seconds. I make it through in 12.52 seconds, which is as slow as I can go without putting a foot down, and I knock over two cones. A pretty poor showing, frankly. My excuse is that I'm still getting used to the Motobi, while everyone else is here on motorcycles they ride all the time. Plenty of locals examine our vintage rides as we scout Bristol's restaurants and then we face our second ability test after the lunch break. This time, at least, I topple only one cone. The third and final ability test of the day comes when we return to the inn. On my third and final try of the day, I topple no cones, but I still can't ride slow enough to be a threat to any of the real competitors.

Make no mistake. Some of these riders really want to win this thing. The Motogiro competitors are good people, quick to lend a wrench or share spare parts or help with a parking lot repair, and they all inevitably say they're just here to have fun. But even as they say it, you catch a glint in the eye that reveals more. After all, most of the USCRA's events are true road course races, and some of the members, such as Frank Camillieri, have legitimate racing pedigrees. Camillieri once finished fifth as a privateer in the 1967 Canadian 250cc Grand Prix, which sounds a lot better when you note that three of the four men who finished ahead of him were Mike Hailwood, Phil Read and Yvon Duhamel. Even the non-racers have a streak of competitiveness that's not far below the surface. You see it on the road during the Motogiro in the way some of the 250cc-class riders will put a well-timed pass on a couple of un-suspecting cruiser riders out sightseeing below the speed limit. Sure, the Motogiro guys are only going 55 mph and nobody was trying to *prevent* them from passing, but like all riders with a drop of racing in their blood, they're grinning in their hel-mets knowing they made the pass, despite giving up thirty-five years and 1200cc.

Even if, like me, you have no hope of finishing atop the standings in the ability tests and any chance of competitiveness is thus doomed from the start, the Motogiro is still a damn fun motorcycle ride. We sample some of the state's finest motor-cycle roads, such as Appalachian Gap, and a greater number of nearly anonymous dirt lanes that take us past tumbling New England streams with the bright leaves of fall fluttering into them on a sunny day. Our mid-day stop on the second day is the Tunbridge World's Fair, an event that has been going on virtually uninterrupted for 150 years and where farmers still bring in their most massive draft horses to compete for blue ribbons while the kids crash bumper cars. (This year, the Tunbridge World's Fair has also added the dubious spectacle of a Motogiro ability test as we wobble through cones in the loamy soil of the horse track in front of a surprisingly populated grandstand.) But it wouldn't be a Motogiro if I reached the finish with no trials or tribulations. And sure enough, on the second afternoon of the Giro, as I climb through forested curves of one of those bucolic country roads, Vermont Route 132, the Motobi sputters, stumbles and falls silent.

I coast back downhill to a roadside pull-off I've just passed, put the bike on the center stand and ponder. The lights work, no more dimly than usual. I can see gas in the fuel line leading to the carburetor, but a few kicks fail to yield the usual reliable response. In the silence, I hear the trickling sounds of a New England stream tumbling down the hill. Birds chirp in the shady forest. This would probably be a pleasant spot, I imagine, if I weren't stuck here on a non-running thirty-nine-year-old motorcycle I know nothing about. For lack of a better plan, I turn the Motobi's key, give it another kick and it fires on the first try, just like always. I have no idea what just happened, but I'm off and riding again. Then, as I turn down a dirt road, the Motobi dies again. This time, I have enough clues to form a theory. The vibration of riding on the rough dirt road tips me off.

The Motobi's "key" is not a key like you'd imagine today. It's just a stick of cheap metal with tabs on the end. Turn it ninety degrees and it depresses a plunger that turns on the ignition. The vibration of riding on the dirt road let the key turn and cut off the ignition. With that figured out, the Motobi is again a reliable companion. If it doesn't start on the first kick, I know to jiggle the key. I once read comments by a psychologist to the effect that satisfaction comes not from having an easy life with no setbacks, but from facing challenges we're capable of overcoming. A loose key is just about the right level of challenge to match my mechanical expertise. I ride onward a happy man.

After the last ability test at the Tunbridge World's Fair (no foot dabs, no toppled cones . . . yes!) the ride is pretty much a straight route back to the inn where the points will be tallied and the winners announced. With an open stretch of road ahead, for the first time in my motorcycling life I ride five miles with the throttle wide open, never once backing off, yet never in danger of getting a speeding ticket.

Once the awards have been presented, the winners congratulated, and bold promises made about better performances next year, the Motogiro riders begin drifting off. I track down Strempfer to help him load the Motobi 125 into his trailer, but she's already been packed up. I hardly had a chance to say goodbye.

Ciao, bella. Thanks for the memories.

JUST THE RIGHT PLACE,
EXACTLY THE RIGHT TIME

*Nobody goes to Tuxpan, which is the main
reason I went there. As it turned out, that
night in December, it was the best place in the
world I could be.*

Nobody goes to Tuxpan, which is the main reason I went there.

Sometimes, usually when I'm traveling for enjoyment with somebody else or traveling for "work" (writing a magazine story about a specific site, for example), I focus on a Destination with a capital "D." By that I mean a place distinguished by natural beauty, by historical or cultural importance, by its fun quotient, or by some other unusual feature that draws people. When I'm traveling by myself, for purposes of regeneration, recreation, and perhaps a little enlightenment, I avoid "Destinations." It's not that I don't know where I'm going, it's that I don't fully know in advance what I'm going to find when I get there, because I tend to choose places lacking in obvious attractions.

There are several benefits, for me, at least, of travel to destinations that don't have a capital "D." For one, it's the only way I've ever gained any real knowledge of the lives of the people who live there. Imagine a foreign visitor coming to see the United States, hoping to do more than just see a few famous sights. He wants to increase his understanding of us as a people and get an idea of how we actually live, beyond what's depicted in the sensational Hollywood films and imported television shows that come into his home. Where is a foreign tourist most likely to go? Manhattan? The Grand Canyon? Worse yet, Las Vegas? Would visiting any of these places give him much insight into your personal life? Probably not, unless you happen to be part of the 0.7% of the U.S. population that lives in Manhattan or Las Vegas, or you lead mule expeditions into the Grand Canyon for a living. So why would we think that visiting Cancun would teach us much about Mexico?

Of course most people take foreign vacations to get away from everyday life. Thus the popular vacation activity of lying semi-lifeless on a beach in an all-inclusive resort. Nothing wrong with that, as everyone's entitled to the vacation of their choice, means permitting. But in my experience, people in search of that kind of vacation are unlikely to arrive via motorcycle. Those of us who take the trouble to ride to small-D destinations are probably seeking out, rather than avoiding, immersion in new and foreign surroundings.

I arrived in Tuxpan, in the Mexican state of Veracruz, aboard an eight-year-old single-cylinder motorcycle with more than 40,000 miles on the odometer, so it was clear even to a casual observer that I was not in search of the sort of ease and comfort represented by a first-class airline ticket, quickly followed by a beach chair and a mai tai. There's no beach in

Tuxpan anyway, unless you count the banks of the river of the same name, and that waterfront is geared more toward shipping grain and servicing the ships that tend to the offshore Pemex oil drilling platforms than to beach chairs and fruity drinks. Tuxpan did have a comfortable and affordable (low cost is another benefit of destinations without a capital "D") downtown hotel with a parking lot nearby with a twenty-four-hour attendant, safe for parking the BMW overnight.

There's an intense feeling of aliveness I get when walking some narrow, cobblestone street in an obscure Latin American city or town. The people around me are immersed in their everyday lives, rushing home from work and anticipating dinner, staring in a store window and weighing the joy versus the expense of buying that toy for a son, aggressively trying to sell just a few more packs of chewing gum or frilly girls' hair barrettes before the evening's last light fades. Far from my own everyday life, I'm able to melt into the background of the everyday lives of others, and the mere act of observance is a learning experience. A place like Tuxpan, where I could walk around the small city for an entire afternoon and hardly see another foreigner, is perfect for that.

It was also a perfect place to take care of necessities after a week on the road, since I'd be spending two nights there, so I found an internet café and sent messages home, surrounded by youths half my age immersed in chat rooms, and then dropped off my dirty clothes (basically all of them, by that point in the trip) at a laundry. A stop at a bakery provided the makings of a simple and inexpensive meal, and a concert by a local band at the park near the river provided the free entertainment while I ate and watched the streetlights pop on above the river.

The next morning, I rode south from Tuxpan to visit a

thousand-year-old archaeological site and afterwards I stopped at one of the tents where women were selling cheap souvenirs. I wanted to buy a couple of T-shirts for my nephews, but the woman didn't have the sizes I needed. She rushed off to one of her fellow vendors, obviously to trade some inventory, while I continued browsing. I was in no hurry on a sunny and warm December day in Mexico, the one day of my trip where I already had my hotel room for the night, where I literally didn't have a bag to pack or unpack or a single deadline to be heeded other than the fall of darkness itself. But the situation was exactly the opposite for her. I looked up to see her running back toward me, clutching some children's T-shirts, near desperation because I might drift away and she would lose a sale amounting to no more than a few U.S. dollars.

"*No hay prisa, señora*," I told her, assuring her I was in no hurry and she need not run, but clearly she didn't feel that way. I bought a T-shirt for each nephew, but the image that stuck most firmly in my mind for many of the miles on the long ride home was not the stone carvings of the ancient site but the face of the winded T-shirt vendor, rushing toward me to salvage a sale on a slow day. All of which made me wonder just how crucial those few pesos were for meeting her goal of feeding her family for another day.

Back in Tuxpan, I was enjoying my last evening of relative relaxation before starting northward for home, but this evening the street scene was different. In addition to the usual street vendors, dozens of women were selling candles on all the downtown streets, and the stores also had them on display. I puzzled over the sudden explosion in candle sales as I walked to the laundry to pick up my clothes, where I talked to the woman who ran the business and her teenage son, who was helping her. He was an aspiring musician and full of questions about whether it was possible to make a living playing music in the United States. You could see all sorts of dreams in his young eyes, dreams likely unfulfilled by working in the family laundry. After I answered all his questions, I had questions of my own, and they explained to me the spike in candle sales. In one of those happy accidents that travel sometimes gifts us, my last night in Tuxpan was *el Día del Niño Perdido,* or Lost Child Day.

It's a unique Tuxpan tradition that dates to the 1800s. Families that had lost a child to death would place candles in front of their houses in remembrance. More than a century later, *el Día del Niño Perdido* is still an enduring public festival observed every December. Those thousands of candles sold by sidewalk vendors were placed along the edges of the sidewalks to line the streets after dark, and all evening adults and teenagers scurried around to relight candles blown out by the breeze. Instead of traffic, the candlelit streets were filled with strolling families. Small children pulled homemade cars and trucks behind them on strings. The little cars, some of them elaborate, resembled the kind of floats made for parades in the United States, only about 1/100th scale. It was a festival not quite like any I'd seen before, anywhere: more sober than most Latin American fiestas, less commercial than U.S. festivals, and utterly unique. Through pure luck, I was in the one place in the world on that December night that I might have chosen to be, if I had even known that such a holiday existed.

The morning after *el Día del Niño Perdido,* I had to head north, the sunshine disappearing behind clouds, my time for travel ending, the time to return to duties at home growing closer, while around me the people of Tuxpan, a place nobody visits, opened their bakeries and laundries and internet cafes and sent their kids to school. In a lucky lifetime, I've been able to visit some spectacular capital-D Destinations, the manmade and natural wonders we are supposed to see, such as the Schönbrunn Palace in Vienna, Glacier National Park in Montana, the Lincoln Memorial in Washington, D.C., and many other "sights." And yes, I've also spent many an enjoyable afternoon in Manhattan, seen the Grand Canyon, and even survived a couple of visits to Vegas. But just as vivid are memories of places that never make anyone's list of Destinations, anonymous little places such as San Vito, Costa Rica, or Nipigon, Ontario, Canada. Usually, those memories stick with me because I not only visited a place, but through chance or planning, got a look into the lives of people who live there—people unlike myself—and learned something in the process.

Such was the case with my sojourn in Tuxpan. I can't describe for you, in any detail, the rooms of the Schönbrunn Palace, though I can assure you that all the ones I saw were opulently spectacular. What I do remember, much better, is the look on the face of the woman rushing to find the T-shirt I wanted before I changed my mind, and how glad I was that I waited. I remember a teenager washing laundry in Tuxpan while dreaming of making a living as a musician in the United States, and hundreds of children pulling homemade *carritos* through candlelit streets in memory of children who did not survive. And most of all I remember the surprising magic of finding myself in the best place I could possibly be on that one night of the year, even though I didn't know enough to choose it on purpose. Sometimes, it works out that way, and a simple motorcycle journey leaves lasting memories of a very human, not historic, scale, from a place where nobody goes. Something to consider the next time you're choosing a destination.

CIRCLING THE HEAD
OF THE WOLF

*The Wolf's Head Tour is a five-day ride
around Lake Superior where you start out
with a group of strangers and finish with a
group of new friends.*

As motorcycle roads go, Route 17 through Lake Superior Provincial Park in Ontario, Canada, exercises the rider's senses more than his or her muscles. Curves are few, views numerous. For a while, the road hugs Lake Superior, offering endless blue to my left toward the western horizon, and pothole lakes, bogs and evergreens to my right. About 100 miles into Canada, I catch up to three motorcycles ahead. I instantly recognize the group, even though I don't yet know any of the riders' names. They're easy to spot. It's not often you see a group consisting of a Suzuki SV650, a Ducati 748 and an eighties-era Honda Silver Wing, and I've seen them several times over the past two days. The four of us have the road to ourselves, and then the 748 rider suddenly points to the roadside and slows. There, chest deep in the foliage, is a cow moose.

We circle back for a second look. I shoot photos from a discrete distance, while the moose munches away, keeping a wary eye on us but tolerating our presence. In quiet appreciation, we admire the sight, a rare one for us south-of-the-border types, until the silence is torn as some guy in a car slams on the brakes and backs up beside the moose for a better look. That's too much attention for her, and she lopes off into the forest. See? Even moose prefer motorcycles to cars. Despite the premature interruption to our wildlife gawking, we still can't help but feel that our "Welcome to Canada" moment is complete.

We spend a few minutes with introductions. The three riders are all in their early twenties, all from the Milwaukee area, and taking their first long-distance motorcycle trip. The Silver Wing rider, Tom Condon, explains with justifiable pride how he bought his old Honda on the cheap and fixed it up, building himself an inexpensive but reliable machine for touring and commuting. After a few more minutes, we ride on toward the town of Wawa, strangers no longer.

Some days, you ride alone. Some days, you ride with friends. Riding alone means setting your own pace, stopping on a whim to check out roadside oddities, starting early if you feel energetic, or calling it quits early if your concentration is waning. Riding with friends means having someone to share dinner with and rerun the day's highlight reel, which is an enjoyable part of the experience in itself, but it also means giving up a lot of the freedom and spontaneity of a solo trip. Almost always, we must choose one or the other. But I've been on one ride that's an exception: the Wolf's Head Lake Superior Circle Tour. An organized, five-day, 1,500-mile ride around Lake Superior, it gives you a choice, sometimes several times in one day. Ride on your own, with friends, or start out on your own and make new friends before the day's over.

The Wolf's Head Lake Superior Circle Tour ran annually for more than a decade in conjunction with the Wolf's Head Rally, though both were canceled in 2009 and a return, of the tour at least, was planned for 2010. Self-guided tours around Lake Superior are a common thing, and you'll even see the "Circle Tour" signs as you ride around the lake. What makes the Wolf's Head tour a little different is that you're joined by a hundred or so other motorcyclists on a scenic route that's been mapped out for you. The year I signed up, we began in the town of Two Harbors, Minnesota. On a crystal clear summer morning, we gathered for the riders' meeting and received our Wolf's Head passports and instructions for how to fill them. The ride may be its own reward, but there's one other memento waiting at the end for those who reach all seventeen checkpoints along the tour's route and get those passports duly stamped: an individually numbered belt buckle.

"If you break down along the way, we'll pick you up in the truck and we'll give you a free registration for next year's tour," Tim Krohn, one of the organizers, tells us. "But you don't get a buckle. You have to ride every inch of the way to get that." These guys are serious about their belt buckles.

Of course the centerpiece of this ride is the big lake itself. Lake Superior's stats are impressive. At 350 miles across and with a maximum depth of 1,333 feet, it holds 10 percent of the entire world's supply of fresh water. But the numbers pale next to reality as I stand on Superior's shore, small against the seemingly endless expanse of sapphire blue, feeling the relentless breeze cooled by fifty-degree water while the rest of the lower forty-eight states swelter in a heat wave. When we stray from the lake shore, it's often to pass through thick forests. In one spot I smell the lingering taint of a long-dead forest fire. For many more miles, I'm immersed in the scents of endless pines and spruces lining the road like green canyon walls, the smell breezing into my helmet as strong as if I've stuffed my face into a Christmas tree decorated with those little pine-scented air fresheners that people hang from their rearview mirrors. Pine overload.

The first day's ride takes us south through Duluth and past hayfields of northern Wisconsin to our first checkpoint at Fish Lipps restaurant in Cornucopia. Next to the restaurant is the Post Office, where a sign announces its status as the northernmost Post Office in the state. With more than a hundred of us stopping in to Fish Lipps to get our passports stamped, we Wolf's Head riders and passengers have increased the little town's population by more than 30 percent. The street is lined with motorcycles, paint and chrome gleaming in the brilliant summer sun.

"Cornucopia hasn't seen the likes of this in a while," a local resident says brightly as she drops a letter in the mailbox.

From there we avoid the through traffic of cars and RVs and pickups pulling fishing boats on U.S. Route 2 and hug the shoreline as much as possible, until we come to the pretty lakeside town of Bayfield, Wisconsin, where the bright sunshine makes both the white hulls of the boats and the colorful baskets of flowers along Main Street glow with unnatural brilliance.

One of my favorite parts of the ride comes on day two, when we venture to the tip of Michigan's Keeweenaw Peninsula, which juts sixty miles into Lake Superior. Traffic is sparse and unhurried on the peninsula. These roads are not on the way to anyplace, so anyone who is here wants to be here. And it's a fine place to be anyway, as I enjoy the contrast of the light blue summer sky, dark blue Superior, and the deep green of the spruces lining the ribbon of asphalt that leads us to Copper Harbor at the peninsula's tip—as close to the center of Lake Superior as you can get without a boat. A sign in Copper Harbor proclaims: "You are now breathing the purest, most vitalizing air on earth." I have no evidence to the contrary.

Each day of the ride begins with a breakfast riders' meeting with tips on the day's route and a few prizes handed out. Then we're free to ride our own pace. But inevitably, we run into each other at checkpoints, at motels at the day's end, and by chance along the road. We're all riding our own tour, but we grow into a traveling community, a loose and constantly shifting formation of riders tracing the outline of the big lake that some say looks like the head of a wolf. One day, I see a row of Harley-Davidson touring rigs with Texas plates parked outside a restaurant and I already know who's inside. Even on the first morning of the tour in Two Harbors, it was easy to spot the Texans. These are big men on big motorcycles. Most, so I heard, are current or former arms of the law: cops, prosecutors and the like. Not sure how they'll accept an outsider, I wander up to their table and they quickly invite me to join them, then resume their normal conversation, which consists of needling each other mercilessly.

"Those two *trailered* their bikes up here," one whispers to me as if sharing a dark family secret. "Us real men rode up from Amarillo."

"Some of us have real jobs and don't have time to ride all the way," replies one of the targets. And so it goes, all through breakfast. In fact, all through the tour.

Darrell Garner, senior member of the group, informs me that he is celebrating both his 62nd birthday and his retirement from law enforcement. His younger friends don't let the opening pass.

"So," one asks, "tell us about the old days. What was pursuit like on a horse?"

The verbal jabs continue as we walk out to our parked bikes, but now it's time to ride and cross over to the Canadian side of Superior. Following my encounter with the moose, and the young Milwaukee riders, I roll into Wawa, Ontario. The little towns of Wawa and Nipigon, our two overnight stops on the north side of the lake, seem to have hospitality competition going on. In Wawa, we're offered free camping and a fine picnic dinner. In Nipigon, locals set up a tent to greet us, point us toward our campgrounds and motels, help us find a place to wash clothes or buy supplies, and make sure we have the directions to the cookout that they've planned for us at the lakefront park, complete with music. In addition to the friendliness, the two towns share a fondness for wildlife statues. Wawa is a variation of the indigenous word for "goose," and the town boasts the world's largest statue of a Canada goose. Up the road in Nipigon there's a giant statue commemorating the capture of a world record square tail trout. But I have questions about another kind of roadside marker I've seen dozens of times today.

Proving my ignorance on my first trip to Canada, I ask the friendly locals to enlighten me about the rock-pile statues I've seen alongside the highway and they explain the history and Inuit traditions behind *inuksuks*. These stacks of stones, sometimes shaped to look like a small person, were originally built by the Inuit on the featureless tundra of northern Canada to direct travelers toward the safe paths. They could also be built to point out a good fishing spot or mark a cache of food. Today, people build them along the highways to keep alive the old tradition.

On the last day of the circle tour, as I cross the border back into the United States, I'm wrongly thinking that the best is now behind me. Instead, I learn the charms of Minnesota's North Shore. I make a rest stop at Temperance State Park and stretch my legs by making a short hike to one of its waterfalls. At Palisade Head, I'm stunned by another majestic view of the lake, as dramatic as anything I've seen on the entire trip. I watch as half a dozen rock climbers suspended above oblivion scale the sheer cliff that rises from the water's edge. Their bright blue or yellow helmets help me spot them in the distance as they inch along the vertical crevasses. And some people call *me* adventurous just because I ride a motorcycle.

Then, I make an inland detour to see the International Wolf Center at Ely, Minnesota. This non-profit center is dedicated to educating humans about a species that is more often the subject of fear or hatred or sensationalistic rumor than calm, rational consideration. The exhibits provide facts about the animals, and you can observe the "ambassador wolves" that reside at the center because they can no longer live in the wild. The facility also supports research on wild wolves, and that's one reason it's located in northern Minnsota, which has the largest such population in the contiguous forty-eight states. From Ely, it's a pleasant ride through evergreen forests back to the lake and south to Two Harbors, where my fellow Circle Tour riders are steadily trickling into the fairgrounds. After five days, I recognize most of the faces, even if I don't know all the names. My Wolf's Head passport is checked and I get that you-have-to-earn-it belt buckle, number 369 in my case. My circle tour is done.

Even though I've only traced its wolf's head silhouette, Lake Superior has come up with plenty of surprises for me. Because so little water flows into and out of Lake Superior in comparison to its immense size, experts say it takes two centuries for the water to completely turn over. On the human time scale, that means it's hardly changing at all. It also means that while I've been riding for a few days with new friends, I can count on coming back to Lake Superior any time and I'll always find a familiar friend.

100 AND ONE DETOUR

*Motorcyclists talk about roads the way wine
critics talk about the subtleties of their favorite
pinot noir. And some of the best ones are
found by accident.*

Most people in cars don't talk much about roads, except perhaps to complain about the one they're on at the time, if it has too many potholes or too much traffic. For motorcyclists as well, there are plenty of times when the road beneath our tires is nothing more than useful public infrastructure, a smoothed path between home and work, between the hardware store and the pharmacy errand, between where we are and where we need to be. But when we ride, I mean when we *really* ride, the road becomes so much more. Maybe nobody outside the Department of Public Works pays more attention to roads than we seriously addicted motorcyclists. We talk about roads the way the members of a wine club talk about cabernet and shiraz and the release of this year's Beaujolais nouveau—their subtler nuances, their appealingly unique characteristics, their lamentable shortcomings. Some riders share favorites sparingly, the way serious cooks hand over family recipes: as a gift, and only to the right people, the kind who will appreciate the gesture. There are half a dozen websites I've seen (and unknown numbers I haven't seen) devoted to listing roads that provide the most fun for riders. One of the staples of these "great roads" websites, as well as the bucket lists of best roads occasionally compiled by the motorcycle and car magazines, is Vermont Route 100. No surprise then, that it was on my list of roads to ride someday, long before I finally got the chance to head north on a Suzuki DL650 V-Strom a few summers ago.

In my view, one of Route 100's principal assets is that it winds through Vermont. The people of Vermont have two attributes I truly appreciate: They're a little quirky and they're not excessively numerous. The quirkiness adds interest and the scarcity leaves room for things like mountains and trees and uncrowded backroads. Route 100 wanders through the middle of all this goodness, running nearly the entire north-south length of the little state. Roads such as Interstate 89 and U.S. 7 offer roughly parallel opportunities for mundane transportation for people who just want to get where they're going. That leaves Route 100 primarily for locals and sightseers and those of us who want to experience the ride, not just get it over with.

In the southern part of the state, you can tell this is a weekend getaway road within reach of a major metropolitan area (Boston, in this case) from the number of antique stores, gift shops and ice cream stands. It's entertainingly quaint to look at for a while, but better riding lies farther north, where Route 100 traces the eastern edge of the Green Mountain National Forest and the road's course appears to be determined more by natural features, such as streams and mountain ridges, than by manmade concerns. All of this is very scenic, from the neatly polished little New England towns that slow me down just long enough for them to draw my admiring glance, but not long enough to make me feel I'm mired in traffic, to the forested slopes and valley farms. In Vermont, a black-and-white Holstein cow motif is the state color scheme, and Route 100 plays along with the bucolic, laconic image. Just as the small towns don't cause enough urban-style traffic to induce angst, nor are the curves sharp enough for me to work up a sweat. Instead, they lull me into the relaxed rhythm of a cruising pace.

Around one of those sweeping turns I find a faded 1976 Honda CB550 Four parked in a wide spot by the road, its owner crouched at its side. I stop to see if I can provide assistance or, more likely, given my mechanical skills and the near absence of tools on the V-Strom, provide company and commiseration. The rider tells me that he only recently pulled the old Honda out of storage and is still tracking down electrical problems, one of which has just left him at roadside. While we examine fuses and poke at the thirty-year-old patina of corrosion on the ground wire, he asks me about my ride and I explain my northward course on Route 100 and my general lack of plans more detailed than that.

"You should ride Lincoln Gap," he advises. "You won't believe it. You just go up and up the mountain."

About that time, the Honda's lights come back on, though it's hard to say what we did to achieve that success. I suspect it won't be his last search for wayward electrons in the old bike. While he sputters off southward toward home, I continue north, not giving our conversation a lot of thought. But his words stick somewhere in the back of my mind and after 100 miles on Route 100 something else is gnawing away at what should be a fine day of riding. I'm on a road known for being one of New England's more scenic rides. The V-Strom 650 (or "Wee-Strom," as its many fans affectionately call it) is, in my opinion, at the same time one of the more homely bikes produced in recent years and also the single most versatile motorcycle you can buy. It provides wind protection and comfort suitable for long-haul blasts on the interstate and still handles nimbly on a tight and twisty two-lane. The engine is Suzuki's jewel of a 650cc V-twin. But beyond all that, with its heavily grooved 19-inch front tire and dirtbike ergonomics, the small V-Strom makes a great platform for an adventure-tourer, able to cover long distances even when some of them aren't paved. So what's the problem? Riding the gentle turns of Route 100, it all seems just a little too easy. I feel like the bike's just yawning, and as pleasant as everything is, I'm in danger of doing the same.

The solution pops up at roadside in the form of a sign announcing the turnoff to Lincoln Gap. Just about the time I spot the sign, I finally catch up with the scattered remnants of a tropical storm that wandered into New England and stalled over the Green Mountains, and the first few drops of rain speckle my faceshield. It's mid-afternoon, but the temperature has fallen into the sixties, and looking up the slopes, I see the clouds hanging lower on the hillsides than they have been all day. I'm not sure if the road over is paved. I forgot to ask the CB550 rider and the squiggles on my map are too small to provide a reliable answer. Thus, I have a choice. Ahead lies easy riding on the smooth and gentle pavement of Route 100. The other way lies an unknown detour with questionable conditions, falling temperatures and looming rain. Really, it's no choice at all. I bank left onto the road up Lincoln Gap, and it feels like the V-Strom wakes up from its nap.

Not long after I turn off Route 100, the road begins switching between pavement and hard-packed mud and gravel. The rain begins falling steadily as I climb, but the V-Strom shrugs off the conditions. At a trailhead parking spot atop the mountain, a sign announces the elevation, 2,424 feet. Four young guys are preparing to hike the trail in the drizzle and I ask them to pause and take a photo of me with the bike, "so I have proof I was stupid enough to come up here in the rain."

"Hey, we're here too," one of them says, while reaching for my camera.

We ponder this simple truth in a silent moment of brotherhood, the few, the not-so-proud, the ones who go out in the rain on purpose. Then they're off on the trail and I begin my descent from Lincoln Gap.

As is generally the case, going down proves to be harder than going up, in part because the pavement soon ends but the rain doesn't. Despite its adventure-touring abilities, the V-Strom demands a little respect and caution on wet, rippled, pot-holed dirt roads. At least that's the case if, like me, your total off-pavement riding amounts to a fraction of one percent of your lifetime mileage. True dirt riders would scoff at such concerns and easily handle the conditions, but I'm carefully feeling out every bit of feedback each time I have to brake for another muddy hairpin, alternating between the slick, hard-packed mud in the tire tracks and the sloppy gravel in between to find the best traction of the moment. By the time I reach the bottom, the bike and I are splattered on the outside with mud and road spray, though my gear has kept me dry and comfortable on the inside. And neither the V-Strom nor I are yawning.

Better yet, when I reach pavement once again, I find that my detour has dumped me onto Vermont Route 17, a smoothly paved two-lane that climbs over Appalachian Gap as it returns me to Route 100. My unexpected side trip has given me a pleasant surprise in the form of a great road. I couldn't help imagine how much more fun it would have been on a dry day with loads of traction, but the rain did have its benefits: It quickly cleaned the worst of the Lincoln Gap mud off the V-Strom's semi-dual-sport tires, which had proven themselves off pavement and were now doing an admirable job of gripping wet asphalt, and it also fed the roadside streams to overflowing, creating a thundering roadside waterfall among the lush greenery of mid-summer Vermont to entertain me.

There's an old saying that adventure begins when things stop going according to plan, which may well be true. But in our modern, everyday world, with thousands of rules and devices and innovations to keep us safe and comfortable, "adventure" is a highly overused word, applied to everything from trying a new restaurant to taking your kids to the amusement park. Certainly, nothing about my ride through Vermont constitutes true adventure. Dirt riders would have shrugged at the relatively mild challenges of a rainy Lincoln Gap, and local street riders would hardly consider my personal discovery of Routes 100 and 17 to be anything new. They're well known local favorites.

My point is, it wasn't adventure that began when things stopped going according to plan, but a good deal of fun did.

For a long time, I'd planned to cross Vermont Route 100 off my list of roads to ride, but in the end, my memories of Lincoln Gap's slick mud and Appalachian Gap's streaming-wet pavement are far more vivid. And I have to give credit to a chance word of advice from a local and my own bias that the best moments often arise not from the best-laid plans, but the detours from those plans. I'm glad that old Honda's electrics chose to go on the blink when they did.

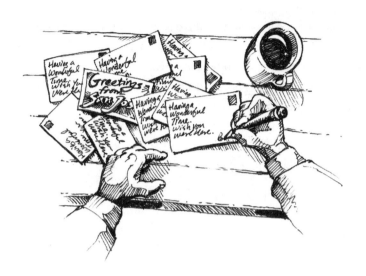

CHARACTERS

*You meet all kinds of people when you're on
the road on your motorcycle. The kind you
never meet while sitting on the sofa at home.*

Surprised to find the doors of the little roadside *colmado* store
open on a sleepy Sunday, I banked the motorcycle into the two-
car parking lot and we went inside to find something to beat
down our thirst. The owner fetched cold drinks from his old-
style chest cooler as we admired the distant view of the Atlantic
coast from this little road perched high in Puerto Rico's
Luquillo Mountain Range. While we cooled off and enjoyed
the view, the storekeeper began telling an old tale. He pointed
toward a spot in the mountains and told us of an ancient cave
there marked with symbols left by the Tainos, the island's pre-
Columbian inhabitants. Some thirty years earlier, his father,

brother and two uncles hiked along a jungle-choked ridge for three hours from the nearest road to reach the cave, where they descended with ropes, down through room after room, until they ran out of line and had to climb back out. The goal of the expedition was to search for a treasure supposedly stashed in the cave by legendary Puerto Rican pirate Roberto Cofresí. Through a little more than sixty years of life, the storekeeper told us, he had never reached that cave himself, though he could see the spot from his front door and he still hoped to get there some day.

I imagine it was a story the old man had told many times, and it was entertaining despite its total implausibility. Why would Cofresí have hidden his treasure deep in a cave and high on a mountain on the opposite corner of the island from the coast where he normally plied his trade? But thinking too deeply about those realities, or thinking at all about the true odds of the storekeeper ever acting on his dream of rappelling into that cave, given his age, would have only diminished his story. So we chose not to, and we rode on with far more than our thirst satisfied.

I don't remember another specific detail about the ride my wife and I took that Sunday afternoon, but I still remember the old man telling his story. It's one of those quirks of humanity that define us. We may love motorcycles with an enthusiasm severe enough to qualify us for a clinical study. We may suffer an addict's craving for the physical sensations of riding. We see some of the earth's greatest sights on two wheels, and experience them more intensely because we ride to them. Yet because we are human, the most memorable part of many a ride is neither the destination nor the journey, but some unexpected character met along the way.

If you happen to own a motorcycle bearing the logo of one of the resurrected marques, such as the Triumph I often ride, you're guaranteed to have extra conversations on the road. It happens to me time and again. An older man approaches me at a gas station to exclaim, "I didn't know they were still in business!" Then he tells me about the old Bonneville he had back in the day, and at some point his gaze drifts off to some unfocused place, and I can just hear him thinking, wondering, trying to remember why he ever sold that old motorcycle. Sometimes, any motorcycle will do to spark such a wistful conversation. Once I stopped for gas in upstate New York on a Suzuki V-Strom and the out-of-state license plate was enough to trigger the forty-something guy coming out of the convenience store to run over to me, ask cursorily where I was from, and then launch into an excited monologue about a cross-country motorcycle trip he took in his twenties, one of those life-altering experiences that's never forgotten, even though he'd hardly ridden since. His tale didn't slow down long enough for me to get a word out, which was good, because the obvious question was one I didn't have the heart to ask: "Why did you stop?" Why did that experience have to be just once-in-a-lifetime? Maybe I was imagining it, but there seemed to be some sadness punctuating the end of his story of excitement, youth, and adventure. He never really asked a word about where I was going, or why. He was still running on the fumes of a ride that was twenty years in the rearview mirror and I had places to go that very same evening. I rode away feeling a little sorry for him, as I do occasionally for the men who tell me about long-lost Triumphs and Harleys and Indians, and I promised myself yet again not to travel down the road to regrets, if I can help it.

Characters. There was the old man I came across in Kentucky who had traveled the country with his wife of 50 years in an RV until she died. Then, when his home without her quickly became unbearable, he took to the road with even greater intensity, taking buses and planes to all the states, all of Canada, and then on to Europe, in constant motion as if afraid to stop. Alone on the road was an adventure. Alone at home was more than he could stand.

There was the young couple from some northern state (I now forget which one) that I ran into at a convenience store next to the interstate somewhere between Daytona Beach and Orlando, with no home, no job, little money, few prospects. Basically, they had each other, a small duffel bag with a few items of clothing and—the young man let me know with a peek into his bag—a .45-caliber handgun, just in case. They had only the vaguest of plans: to find a town with enough social services to sustain them long enough to find a job and try to build something of a life, starting from as darn near close to zero as you can get. People stopping on their way home from work or just trying to get back on the interstate and make time rushed past them, in and out of the store, avoiding eye contact in the sickly artificial roadside glare as darkness threatened to fall. Based on no more than a short conversation with me, a total stranger, they decided to cast their fate toward Daytona Beach, not Orlando, and began trying to hitchhike a ride on the eastbound side of I-4 instead of the westbound side. Once again, I rode on, glad to be on my life's road instead of another.

These are ordinary people, caught in lives and travels that I recognize, gratefully, are different from mine. I've also met some famous people through motorcycling, from professional racers to people in the entertainment business, but it seems like the anonymous, desperate types are the ones that lodge most firmly in my memory, like characters from a Steinbeck novel.

Of course, because I stop for fellow motorcyclists stranded alongside the road, I've also met riders who ran out of gas, who are waiting for a tow truck or the friends they called on a cell phone for help, and at least one who rode into a ditch and was waiting for his riding buddies to realize he was no longer behind them and come back to help him haul his motorcycle out of the spot where it was stuck. Surprisingly often, there's a little humor found in those roadside encounters, but they can also be grim. I once pushed a car-shattered motorcycle off a busy city avenue, while the medics attended to the rider, because I was the only one among the little crowd of Good Samaritans who stopped to render aid who knew how to get it out of gear so it would roll freely. It wasn't much but it was all I could do. I stop for stranded riders because I've been the beneficiary of kindness many times myself, and from all kinds of people, not just fellow riders. There was the guy with the shop making customized campers who interrupted his work and drove several miles to fill his gas can for me when I foolishly ran out on the highway, or, when I was a college student traveling on a shoe-string budget, the family at the campground that set up their extra tent for me after someone stole some of my camping gear, leaving me without shelter as a night-long rain moved in. It sometimes seems to me that the farther from home, the better people treat me as a traveler and the more they go out of their way to help me out of a jam.

Some people test the kindness of strangers much farther from home than I've ever been. Nearly twenty years ago, when I saw a weathered BMW R100GS Paris-Dakar parked in the courtyard of the hostel in San José, Costa Rica, and the equally weathered guy in dusty motorcycle boots sitting by himself at a table and writing postcards, it wasn't hard to put who and two together. So I intruded on his task and started a conversation. He was a motorcycle messenger in London with a relentlessly restless need to see the world and a simple but brutally demanding plan to accomplish it. For eighteen months, he would live in voluntary poverty, working as many hours as possible, fighting his way through London traffic in the chill and gloom of the old sod, spending not a single pence unnecessarily. Then, when he'd saved enough, he'd take off for a year or two, following routes he'd plotted on maps in the spare minutes of his long work days. His first trip took him across Europe, through India and on to Australia. On the next one, he circled North America. I ran into him on his third and most ambitious trip yet. He had already ridden the length of Africa, north to south, and South America, south to north, to reach Central America. He was in the final phases of this journey before returning to London.

Today, there are thriving websites such as Adventure Rider and Horizons Unlimited where world travelers share updated information and post stories and photos of their trips, sometimes far more elaborate than the stories and photos you see in the glossy magazines. But back in the early 1990s, those resources didn't exist. The traveling Brit I met was finding his own way around the continents. It wouldn't have been as big a challenge as Ted Simon riding his Triumph around the world in the 1970s, a story that would become the book *Jupiters Travels,* or Robert Fulton crossing Asia and the Middle East on his motorcycle in 1932, or Effie Hotchkiss and her mother, Avis, becoming the first women to ride coast to coast across the United States in 1915, when roads hardly existed in much of

North America. But a challenge it was. When I suggested as much, he shrugged it off. There are always people doing something crazier, he said, and he'd encountered many, from young couples that had been traveling the world non-stop for ten years, even having children while living rootlessly, to more than one motorcycling dreamer plotting a ride to one remaining place where no one had ever gone. All of them more anonymous than the dozens of people traveling the world today and documenting their trip at advrider.com, or movie stars geared up with equipment provided by sponsors and setting off on cross-continent excursions with a medical team in the support truck, a camera crew documenting each difficult sand wash and every harsh sunset over the campsite, and "fixers" smoothing the way ahead at border crossings.

At the moment I interrupted his work, the Brit in San José was writing a letter to a family he'd met by chance in Venezuela and had subsequently spent Christmas with. He'd seen more of the world, and from closer up, than most of us would ever imagine. Yet it was no coincidence what he was doing when I approached him. He was staying in touch. He'd already learned that even if you ride around the world and see the most amazing sights this varied and fantastic globe has to offer, what you will remember most are some of the characters you met, totally unexpectedly, along the way.

DREAM RIDING IN
BOOMTOWN

*Riding most race tracks feels like a
particularly sweet slice of the motorcycling life.
Riding Losail International Circuit in Qatar
feels like a sweet slice of a motorcycling
dreamscape. Not quite real at all.*

In dreams, racetracks have no bumps.

As I completed another lap of the Losail International Circuit outside of Doha, Qatar, the experience felt surreal, very much like a dream. The grass bordering the asphalt was too perfect, too uniformly green and even. The sky was not really blue, but a light gray. As I banked the Kawasaki Ninja ZX-10R into the final righthand turn leading onto the long front straight, I skimmed my knee puck with a level of ease and comfort that matched my riding in dreams far better than my skills in real life. And there were no bumps.

Then American roadracer Kenny Noyes, who was born in Spain and currently races for Antonio Banderas in Moto2, whooshed past with ease as he outbraked me into the corner, the rear tire of his ZX-10R slewing side to side slightly, but perfectly under control. Then he disappeared.

Okay. So this is not a dream. In my dreams, I'm not passed *that* easily.

No, not dreaming. I really was riding at Losail in one of the more unexpected opportunities to fall my way. Like a golf fanatic getting an invitation to play a round at Augusta National, or a rabid Boston Red Sox fan winning a pair of free tickets to a World Series game at Fenway Park, I found myself on short notice in a unique place I never thought I'd be, riding a Kawasaki ZX-10R at the world press introduction at Losail. At home in the United States, I've ridden on tracks from Mazda Raceway Laguna Seca in the west, to Road Atlanta in the south, to the Mid-Ohio Sports Car Course a few miles from my home. Each of them felt like a particularly sweet slice of the motorcycling life, but real life none the less. Riding at Losail felt like a sweet slice of a motorcycling dreamscape. Not quite real at all.

Of course there are perfectly good explanations for the surrealism. The "grass" is so uniformly even because it is actually artificial turf, placed alongside the track to prevent at least some of Qatar's incredibly fine sand from blowing onto the racing surface. The odd color of the sky comes from billions of airborne particles of the same sand. My enhanced ability to skim a knee can be credited to the handling capabilities of the Kawasaki, the superior grip of the World Supersport-spec Pirelli tires developed especially for this track, and the perfect condition of the asphalt beneath me. That unnatural smoothness of the track also makes perfect sense, when you know the back story. It's what you get when a small country with massive quantities of petro-dollars to spend sets out to built the perfect motorcycle racing venue.

In the United States, most of our tracks that host professional motorcycle races were built years ago with cars in mind, then subsequently modified in grudging and piecemeal fashion to try to maintain a minimally acceptable level of safety for motorcycles, which get faster every year and therefore need ever larger margins for error. The best new race circuits built in the United States in recent years, such as the Barber Motorsports Park and Miller Motorsports Park, have been the projects of wealthy individuals with a passion for motorsports and a stubborn insistence on doing things right, rather than sliding by with just good enough, which means safety for the riders and an enjoyable experience for the spectators were both considered from the beginning of the design phase. Losail is an altogether different case, an example of a small country with money to spend and a desire to raise its profile in the world and carve new roles for itself. Qatar (locals pronounce it like the word "cutter," though the rest of the English-speaking world seems to insist on calling it "ka-TAR") is a small peninsula, like an appendage of Saudi Arabia, jutting into the Persian Gulf. A British protectorate until it gained independence in 1971, Qatar's wealth comes from its oil and natural gas deposits, particularly the latter. But the country is trying to diversify its economy, and while tourism is only a small part of that plan, it doesn't hurt, when you're a small place that most people know little about, to have millions of people around the world watching a MotoGP and a World Superbike race beamed from your country twice a year. To that end, Losail was built in less than a year at a cost of about $58 million and meets both FIA and FIM international standards. The track debuted in 2004, then Qatar upped the ante and lit the entire track so it could host the first-ever nighttime MotoGP race in 2008.

Look at a satellite photo of Losail and it's almost the same as looking at a drawing of a track map. The aerial view shows the black ribbon of asphalt outlined with green artificial turf, crisply visible on the plain, soft-brown background of desert soil. Situated in an empty area of desert north of the main city of Doha, there is nothing else around it except the highway from the capital. In the view from space, the Persian Gulf appears close by, but on the ground, from the track, there's no hint that you're near the sea. The utter flatness means every view extends the same distance.

Everything at Losail is modern, clean and new, from the garages to the track cafeteria. In the United States, we think track food is, at best, a bratwurst at Road America. I don't know what they serve in the stands on race day, but the cafeteria in the infield at Losail, where we ate, rivaled the best Middle Eastern restaurant in my city back home.

And then there's the lack of bumps.

Actually, the track wasn't perfectly smooth. Losail's feature-less flatness makes one turn look perilously like another, making it easy for an ordinary track-day guy like me to get confused about which turn is coming up next, choose the wrong line or gear and generally botch forward progress. Reference points are few in a flat, treeless desert. But back in the shade of the garages between sessions, everyone nodded and knew which turn we were talking about when someone said, "You know, the turn with the bump."

Right. There's only one of those.

I've never ridden another track that had just one bump.

When not at the track, I spent hours wandering Doha's souk, the sprawling marketplace, and bought gold jewelry to take home to my wife. In the evening, we cruised Doha Bay on a traditional dhow as the sun set behind the city skyline, which consists half of high-rises and half of construction cranes, as more buildings are raised to meet the need for housing of foreign guest workers. Fewer than a million people live on the peninsula and less than half of those are native Qataris. The majority are foreign workers from India, Pakistan, Iran and elsewhere, here to seek work in a country with one of the highest per capita incomes in the world. The result is a very diverse society that still breaks down into just two tiers in most cases, native and foreign. There's occasional abuse and friction that can result when two humans live side by side but have different legal, social, and economic standing, based merely on where they happened to be born. With a U.S. passport bearing a short-term visa in my pocket, I was a detached visitor, somewhere between the privileged Qataris and the masses of guest workers. And anyway, I had my own agenda, one that few of the privileged locals and none of the foreign workers would experience. I was there to ride, to strive to improve my humble riding skills and to evaluate, as much as those modest skills allowed, Kawasaki's new liter bike.

It was a most unexpected agenda. Seriously lacking in the youth and ability I would need to land a World Superbike or MotoGP ride, I certainly never expected to leave a few molecules of my knee pucks at the same Losail International Circuit where Valentino Rossi and Casey Stoner battle. That's something I thought I'd do only in my dreams, where racetracks have no bumps.

ALMOST HEAVEN
FOR RIDING

Yes, I'm biased, but I believe there are few
better places to take a motorcycle ride than
West Virginia.

I could be on U.S. 50 just east of the Cheat River or maybe U.S. 33 between Franklin and Judy Gap. After looping over the endless ancient Allegheny hills, the road takes a deep breath and prepares for a crossing of one of the larger ridges. The sweeping curves clench into hairpins and switchbacks like a spring coiling tighter to leap the higher ground ahead. The curves stack up the mountainside like they're folded back and forth on themselves, but the lanes are extra wide in each hairpin to accommodate the trucks that must grind up and down these steep routes. Otherwise, the trucks would never make it through the tighter turns without sideswiping a guardrail, or at least dragging gravel from the shoulder onto the pavement. Those widened lanes, a necessity for the trucks, are a luxury for me, as they allow me to choose lines that round off the turns and add another 10 mph to my corner speed.

My tires are new, so I'm confident of the front end's bite on the smooth asphalt as I choose a line, weight the outside peg slightly in each turn, and keep my butt light on the seat as I shift my weight side to side, just a little, just enough for street riding, not hanging off like I would on a track where that all-important margin for error and surprise doesn't have to be quite as large. Back and forth, up and over, and then I top the ridge where the road straightens out to normal West Virginia standards, which is to say that I still encounter few straights more than a quarter of a mile in length. The easier pace allows me to rest my quadriceps, which were just starting to get that good-feeling burn from the workout of shifting my weight over the bike as I ascended the mountainside. The slower pace also allows me to see more of the green forests flowing past me, the tumble-down warrens of mossy rocks under the deep shade of old trees. Beside the ramshackle remains of a one-pump gas station that hasn't seen business since prices were fifty cents a gallon, an old, round Phillips 76 sign, rusting toward monochrome, hangs from a pole like the forgotten subject of a public execution that nobody came to see. Little farms still cling to existence alongside these roads, this one with perfectly ordered rows in its garden, the barn crisply painted, the grass cropped tight against the front porch sidewalk, and that one, with junk cars sinking into mud around a sagging mobile home with rusty streaks on its flanks. Crossing a bridge, I get a long view down a stream: the water flashing silver where it slips over rocks and boulders the color of aged bronze, the trees crowding the bank like friends pressed together at the bar for a drink, their limbs arching like raised toasts to form a canopy of green shade. All of this swooshes by like a rolling slideshow of comfortable images, all things I've seen before, but still waiting for me if I take my glance away from the road for a second to consider them. And look, the road's starting to coil again for a climb up another ridge ahead.

This is a little bit of what riding in West Virginia is like. It's a potent form of motorcycling happiness for me and makes my home state of West Virginia, in my opinion, one of the very best places anywhere to ride a motorcycle. And I openly admit my bias.

There are a million kinds of beauty in this world, and I try to appreciate as many as possible, but I think we are all predisposed to feel a special warmth for scenes of the kind of beauty where we grew up, assuming we felt happy and safe there. So a harsh, dry, and stark landscape at sunset feels comforting to the man who once was a boy growing up in the desert, and the near black and white of snow and pines under weak northern sun seems like quiet shelter to someone who skied through those forests as a child. For me, that feeling of a benign, welcoming scene comes from the eastern North American woodlands in full summer greenness. This is not, I realize, automatically so for everyone. I know people from the city who see those same woods as a forbidding place, vaguely dangerous. Literature from the early colonial era employed dark imagery to describe the forests that stretched unbroken from the Atlantic coast to the plains as the home of evil, and settlers threw themselves into the task of cutting down as much of it as possible to let the sun in. But for me, those woodlands were a gentle boyhood playground, and in a way, they are still a playground today, when I ride through them on a motorcycle.

When I was in second grade, we moved to the city of Columbia, South Carolina where I began a career of being the "new kid" who didn't fit in. When we were given an open-ended art assignment, I, feeling a little homesick maybe, tried to recreate that lush green fecundity on the eight-and-a-half-by-eleven piece of drawing paper I'd been provided as a canvas. My effort depicted the forested hills I remembered with hundreds of trees laboriously and individually drawn, a task that seemed to take forever and, in the end, was completely unsatisfying. I remember my teacher looked at my work and, when I explained the concept, remained silent, no doubt thinking, "If you can't say something nice . . ."

I long ago gave up trying to capture images on drawing paper. The best I can do now is to try to paint the old familiar scenes with words, and while I'm still rarely satisfied with the results, I keep trying. Fortunately, I'm willing to return to West Virginia's near-empty and amazingly smooth back roads on a regular basis for more research.

When traveling alone, I prefer to camp, and that's especially true in West Virginia, where the best attractions nearly all lie outdoors. My wife says luxury is wasted on me anyway, and she's usually right about such things. The truth is that a night by myself in a hotel leaves me feeling vaguely lonely while a night by myself in a campsite feels like welcome solitude. I can't explain the difference. My favorite time for a motorcycle camping trip is in the fall. The campgrounds empty out because school is in session, which keeps families close to home, and the chill in the night air deters the casual campers. Fall provides great riding, too, with a generous share of sunny, dry days and, for a fleeting few weeks, the hills lay out a backdrop of a dozen shades of red, yellow, brown and green.

It's easy to miss the mark with a fall motorcycle camping trip, however. Last year, I saw a forecast for a few sunny days coming around the peak of the leaf change and rode toward Blackwater Falls State Park. At 3,200 feet it doesn't sound all that high, but within twenty miles of the park, I began spotting roofs covered with snow. I'd heard about the early autumn snowfall in central Pennsylvania, but nobody mentioned to me that it had extended this far south. By the time I rode over the last ridge before reaching the park, the trees were fully laden with snow, the road damp in spots with an unsettling sheen to it, and while there wasn't a thermometer in sight, I knew we couldn't be far from the freezing point. I eased into camp using the mildest of lean angles in the curves, set up the tent amid unexpected clumps of white, and settled in for a cooler night than I'd expected, but happy in that rare instance to be done riding for the day. In the morning, I couldn't read the bike's gauges because of the thick frost on the lenses, but the sunshine was unblunted and the forecast called for temperatures near seventy degrees in the lower elevations by mid-afternoon, so I dawdled over coffee on the front porch of Nannys café in Davis, the town next to the park, and watched the sun dry and warm the pavement. During October in West Virginia you may not often get to experience all four seasons in a single day, but three is not altogether unlikely.

West Virginia's near total lack of flatness provides the curves, and years of generously applied federal pork-barrel funding may explain the smoothness of the roads, but there are other, unexpected treats along many of the state's great motorcycle routes. Like riding Route 88's squiggly loops in the northern panhandle, which brings me to Wheeling's Oglebay Park, its old mansion, now a museum, unexpectedly rising at roadside. Or just east of the town of Harmon, pausing on Route 55 where a ridge-top sign announces the Eastern Continental Divide while another sign orders truckers to pull over and check their brakes before beginning the descent that ends with the reward of a dramatic view of Seneca Rocks jutting into the sky, yellow-white in the afternoon sun. U.S. 60's sudden onslaught of 25 mph curves announces the approach of Hawks Nest State Park, perched above the New River Gorge. Near the Snowshoe ski resort, West Virginia Route 66 winds over the mountain and then drops me back a century as I roll into the historic logging town of Cass, where the old company houses have been restored and turned into vacation rental cabins. When my timing is just right, I park by the old Cass station just in time to hear the blast of the whistle as the coal-fired steam locomotive of the Cass Scenic Railroad pulls in to unload sightseers. Briery Gap Road leads me to Spruce Knob, West Virginia's highest point at 4,861 feet. It is more than worth the detour, both for the views from the top and for the fine, winding pavement that gets there in a wiggling series of switchbacks and curves.

There's a road—whose name I don't even know, now that I come to think about it—that leads to what is probably the strangest natural spot in West Virginia. To get there, I seek out Jordan Run Road in Grant County and watch for the sign that points toward the Dolly Sods Wilderness. Having enjoyed my streetbike on West Virginia's smoothly paved curves, now is the moment when I wish I could morph my machine just temporarily into a lightweight dual-sport with knobbies, so I could charge up the mountain. Instead, I lumber. No charging this single-lane, rutted road of dirt and jagged rocks, not on a 500-pound motorcycle with street tires. It's five miles steadily up-hill, first gear all the way, but the destination makes the ride worthwhile. Dolly Sods is a high plateau that looks like a little bit of Canada, fifty miles south of the Mason-Dixon Line. Stunted red spruce trees grow one-sided from the beating they take from the wind, and the bogs and heaths, studded with jumbled boulders, look like nothing you'll find elsewhere in West Virginia. In the 1800s, settlers would burn formerly logged areas to create grazing land they called "sods," and this area was settled by a family named Dahle. From there sprang the odd name, Dolly Sods.

In West Virginia, even the roads that don't offer any partic-ular attraction will still take you for a good ride. Just about any-where on Route 16 is enjoyable, for example, or Route 20 through the heart of the state. In West Virginia, even the inter-states have curves, and they also have 70 mph speed limits, so you notice the curves. Really, it's hard to find a bad motorcycle road in West Virginia, but if you're looking for one, you should start somewhere near my hometown. That's right, my home county along the broad Ohio River Valley probably has more flat and straight roadway than any other part of the state, but even there, I know a few hidden gems.

While you're riding through their state, the people of West Virginia are more likely than not to leave you alone, unless you make the first move, and then they just may smother you with questions and kindness and insist you come home to see Uncle Wilbur's collection of antique tractors, which the less discern-ing eye might confuse with a junk yard, but you will surely ap-preciate because you ride a motorcycle. Just about every small town still has a locally owned lunch counter where you can start your day with a hot breakfast cooked from fresh ingredients, leave the waitress a tip and still get out the door without spending five dollars.

When I return to my home state today, what often strikes me is the boom in the wildlife population. We tend to think of the man vs. nature trajectory going one way only, steadily downhill for nature, but not so in the twenty-first-century Appalachians. This was a thoroughly forested region prior to the 1700s. Then, European settlers hacked out fields for crops and cut trees for cabins and barns. Logging companies followed and clear-cut huge swaths, setting fire to what was left, while mining companies dug and blasted the terrain. Black bears, elk, mountain lions and even wolves, once all native to West Virginia, soon disappeared while a few owners of the logging and mining companies made fortunes. One small town in southern West Virginia called Bramwell was known in the late 1800s for having more millionaires per capita than any other town in the United States. The owners got wealthy, the miners got black lung or crushed by a roof-fall, the loggers wore out early, if they weren't maimed, and the farmers rarely saw much money, but kept at their crops and livestock because they had to eat. My grandfather's lifetime fell into the middle of that brief era of farming, and he, no doubt, will be the last serious farmer in the family line. Today, logging and mining are done in more sustainable fashion and farming in West Virginia is an ancillary activity, with few exceptions. Thus the landscape continues returning closer to what it was in the 1700s, rather than the early 1900s, and wildlife populations are booming. The elk and wolves are still gone, but now I've seen black bears and heard tell of mountain lions. Meanwhile, the animal most dangerous to motorcyclists, the whitetail deer, roams countryside and suburbs alike in brazen herds. It's easy to spot dozens of them in roadside fields on a fall evening, but as any experienced rider knows, it's the one you don't see that will get you.

I could be lots of places. I could be riding in the Rockies or the Alps, and those places make great fodder for bragging about memorable motorcycle rides. Or I could be riding some not-quite-two-lane past the silence of little country church graveyards where my ancestors lie, past the smell of hay drying in the sun, through the coolness that drifts from a deep fold of a shady country holler, back through time, back through re-membrance, pulled along by the motorcycle's torque, which is another remembrance in itself. And I could say, this feels right.

Part 2
Ruminations
& Meditations

FIRST BIKE

*You never forget your first motorcycle. Even if
it was a third-hand, homely, utilitarian
machine that had probably been in a flood.*

At the time, I didn't know that it would mean something years
and decades later. But now, it makes perfect sense that the first
time a legal document was ever filed attesting to my ownership
of something, that something was a motorcycle. Nobody who
met me today would be surprised.

But at eighteen, even the most precocious of us are slates
still mostly blank. And that was the age at which I stumbled
into being a motorcyclist, without much planning, by buying a
very used, non-descript, massively mass-produced bike with a
questionable history (and probably paying too much for it),
falling in love not so much with the machine, but with the
world of sensations and experiences it opened to me.

In other words, pretty much the same old story. Millions of
us did it.

Even today, despite fourteen consecutive years of growth in

sales of new motorcycles in the United States in the 1990s and 2000s, the high point for U.S. sales remains 1973, even though there were about 100 million fewer people in the country then, compared to today. As is so often the case, you can blame or credit demographics. In 1973, the big lump of the Baby Boomer bulge was in young adulthood, prime motorcycling time. At the same time, the Japanese manufacturers were importing relatively inexpensive, easy-to-ride, far-more-reliable motorcycles by the thousands to meet the demand, while Harley-Davidson limped toward its darkest years and the once-mighty British motorcycle industry continued resolutely firing repeated rounds into its foot by building the same old thing, with engines guaranteed to leak oil and headlights likely to fail at the first sign of impending nightfall. Millions of people in the United States at least gave motorcycles a try during that era, and while many drifted off, some caught the addiction and never shook it. And the one thing that absolutely all riders share is a memory, whether dim or vivid, clear-eyed or nostalgic, humorous or heart-warming or traumatic, of a first bike.

For most riders it tends to be something old, something abused, something borrowed or (in my case) something blue. A first bike could be any of thousands of somethings, depending on your age and circumstances. What was yours? A passed-around Indian Scout still soldiering on, years after the Wigwam closed in Springfield, Massachusetts? A Rupp mini-bike with its lawnmower engine that you rode around and around in circles in your parents' back yard until there was a rut deep enough to practice berm shots? A pre-rashed Yamaha FZR600 too cheap to pass up or a hand-me-down Kawasaki Ninja 250 already used as a learning tool by another beginner?

Being in the tail end of the Boomer phenomenon, as usual I

arrived a little late to the party, when the snacks are gone and the punch bowl nearly empty, so I didn't get to participate in the 1973 new-bike buying climax. Instead, I bought one of those bikes that are commonly named as a first motorcycle among my age cohort. In 1979, as a freshman in college, I bought a blue 1976 Honda CB360T for $750, largely because there was no way I could afford to buy or insure a car, and the Honda was the closest I could come to personal transportation. There was nothing remarkable about the Honda. It was a perfect example of what later came to be called the UJM, the Universal Japanese Motorcycle, the do-it-all motorcycles imported by the millions by the Japanese manufacturers in the 1970s before the market became segmented into niches other than displacement size.

It was a "naked" bike before we knew bikes could be dressed. Crude, you might say, from today's perspective. Elemental would be a kinder term. Two spoked wheels, skinny tires, a flat seat for two, and an air-cooled vertical-twin engine. The closest thing to flash it offered was the chromed front fender, a styling touch that was ubiquitous on Japanese motorcycles of that era and which makes absolutely no sense to me when I think about it today. As for the performance package, about the best thing I can say is that it had a disc front brake instead of a drum. I was eighteen and a gullible, unsophisticated consumer by any standards. So these pros and cons, both of styling and performance, slipped by me unnoticed at the time. It would be many years later when I thought to question why the designers wanted to draw so much visual attention to the front fender and came to appreciate that Honda put a front disc brake on the CB360. The seller was pretty gullible, too, or at least trusting, possibly just desperate, because he let me test ride the bike. It was the second motorcycle I'd ever ridden, following my parents' old Honda 50 step-through, which I had only ridden in our country driveway, and thus the CB was also the first motorcycle I'd ridden that had a clutch. Miraculously, I didn't stall it. Thankfully, I didn't crash it. All I did was buy it. I didn't even try to negotiate the price, probably to the seller's surprise. Later, I learned that the motorcycle may have been left at the owner's riverfront camp and at least partially submerged in one of the periodic Ohio River floods. I told you I was eighteen and gullible. In any case, the stone-simple Honda kept running, despite a variety of odd problems that led me to suspect the flood rumors may have been true.

Maybe I have just enough honest memories of what a slug that old bike really was, compared to what we ride today, to explain my behavior when I come across an advertisement for an old CB360 for sale, cheap. I look at the photo, smile and remember, and then I move on. I'm not tempted to try to "relive" my youth. Even if I believed such a thing were possible, I was lucky enough to live through it once.

I survived the old-style method of learning to ride (trial and error, mostly error) largely because I lived in a small town with minimal traffic, and because the Honda's engine couldn't pump out enough power to overwhelm the equally mediocre tires of the era. Where I grew up, motorcycling was about cruising. I fell under little peer pressure to go fast, and the new sensations were exciting enough, to me anyway, even at CB360T speeds. During my college years, I read motorcycle magazines for free in the library and I eventually came across a piece explaining countersteering and began to understand how much more I really needed to understand. It wasn't the ideal way to learn, but it's what we had back then before there were Motorcycle Safety Foundation courses in every state, books and videos on riding well, track-based riding schools taught by former world-champion racers, and even private riding instruction. I learned enough, and was lucky enough, to keep ahead of my ignorance and survive my early years on that CB360T.

Compare my experience as an eighteen-year-old rider to that of an eighteen-year-old living today in, to pick an example, Southern California. On one hand, he's probably a vastly more informed consumer, with magazine shootouts and thousands of internet sites and his friends' opinions to influence him, though he'd probably be better off without some of that "information." Some will tell him, and quite likely convince him, that his first motorcycle should be a late-model 600cc sportbike, so he "won't get bored with it." As he takes his first rides, his throttle hand controls 100 horsepower, about four times what my old CB360T could muster where the rear tire touched the pavement. Miles of eight-lane freeways, either flowing with uncoupled freight trains of 80 mph traffic or halted by congestion, lie between him and any destination. He's led toward temptation by videos of stunters doing standup wheelies, usually on public roads, illegally, flagrantly. Maybe even naked. His friends want to go strafe canyon roads on their even-more-powerful 1000cc sportbikes.

Is it any wonder that kid's life expectancy is less than mine was?

And yet, as much as the world changes, some human sentiments come close to universal. Home from college for the summer, I would park that utterly unremarkable CB360T in the garage of my parents' house after coming in from a night-time ride and listen to the tick ticking of the old air-cooled engine as it dissipated its heat, the metals contracting into their resting places. I could detect the distinct burning smell of oil pooling on the hottest engine parts and the few last wisps of exhaust drifting from the twin exhaust pipes. I lingered in the garage, not wanting to go inside the house. Sitting there, beside that cheap and practical machine few could covet, I savored the ride, even if it was just an ordinary trip across town to a friend's house, and I was, without knowing it, burning deep and lasting memories into a primal part of my brain. The right combination of hot oil on hot metal can yank me back to those moments utterly unexpectedly, decades later.

The experience of today's Southern California kid may be vastly different from mine as a kid in the Ohio Valley of the late 1970s, but it can still plant the same seed. Some of those modern new riders will dabble in the world of motorcycling, then find other interests, whether customized cars or surfing or computer games or simply raising a family and turning away from what they perceive as childish interests. Another few will, unfortunately, be maimed or killed by their inexperience with the powerful motorcycles they can buy, ready or not. Some will be turned away by seeing their friends fall. But a few will probably show even more smarts than I did at that age, will take advantage of the far greater trove of information available today, will make themselves better riders and will survive their first bikes. Then, they'll sit down on a bench in the garage after coming in from a night ride and listen to the sounds of the different alloys of the hot engine clicking as they cool. Those sounds will be different from those of the old, air-cooled motor I owned in the 1970s, but the smell of hot oil or the whiff of burnt hydrocarbons wafting around the exhaust will be similar.

Differences aside, for that young man or woman taking their first motorcycle rides, those sounds and smells and the lingering sensations will plant hooks deep in the most animalistic parts of their brain. Years later those memories will suddenly hit them—maybe over and over for all their lives—and draw them powerfully back to that very moment when they were young and alive and those sensations of riding were as new and vivid to them as the human drives of love and sex and taking deep gulps of the breath of life. And those remembered sounds and smells, like that first bike, will make them motorcyclists for life.

HOW I SURVIVED MYSELF

*Nothing focuses a young man's mind like
gasoline streaming toward his crotch, just
inches from hot engine parts.*

Some time ago I read a book that was a collection of articles, essays and book excerpts on motorcycling. It was clearly designed to capture the attention of people who may or may not actually ride. You can probably imagine the kind of book I'm talking about. The percentage of stories involving the Hells Angels is many times greater than the percentage of Hells Angels among the motorcycling population, and the writers are more famous than me, meaning that although they know less about motorcycles, their names are more likely to sell books.

The most disappointing of those essay was one by Thomas McGuane, a writer whose work of other types I've enjoyed. He recounted how he moved to California, developed an interest in all the motorcycles around him, and bought a brand new Matchless 500 single from a dealership going out of business. A brand new motorcycle he had no idea how to start, much less ride competently. He pushed it home from the dealership in the rain, where he dropped it for the first time before he ever even started it. After some allegedly enjoyable times with the Matchless, he crashed into a car making an illegal U-turn (or, in his words, "had to put the bike down"). Then he sold the motorcycle and returned to his "sensible" car.

For maybe the thousandth time, I was reminded the wisdom of the old adage, "Trust the art, not the artist." I may still enjoy reading a McGuane novel, but in the unlikely event we were ever to sit down and have a drink together, I'd find it very difficult to avoid telling him that anyone who thinks "laying down" a motorcycle is *ever* a good idea, who thinks that a motorcycle skidding down the road out of control with its metal parts gouging the asphalt is preferable to a motorcycle that's upright and braking hard on its grippier tires, is not just a fool, but a dangerous fool, albeit dangerous first and foremost to himself. Such a discussion would probably not make for friendly bonding over a beer.

Though to be honest, I'm not in the best position to criticize McGuane. It's not like I can say that I've never been young and foolish, underinformed and poorly prepared for the demands of riding. I can't even say I've never laid a bike down, though I'm honest enough to admit that when the car made a left turn in front of me, I failed to brake properly and dropped the bike. I didn't *have* to lay it down, I *shouldn't* have laid it down, I just did, due to human error. And that's nowhere near the beginning, end, or height of my ill-advised actions over the years.

Sometimes I talk with my fellow motorcyclists of a certain age and we wonder how we survived ourselves during our first years on two wheels. Those were the days before Motorcycle Safety Foundation courses, Riders Edge training, and shelves full of books and videos on proper riding techniques. Today, serious motorcycle publications have been known to devote pages and pages to debates over the fine points of the MSF curriculum. When I started riding, the curriculum available to most riders consisted of an uncle or an older brother or a dealership salesman saying "This is the clutch, this is the brake, one down and four up," and a slap on the back for good luck. It's quite possible the "advice" also included "Don't ever touch that front brake. She'll throw you right over the handlebars."

When I bought the first motorcycle I could actually call my own, at eighteen years of age, I rode with a second-hand helmet and an old pair of aviator goggles a friend had found during a particularly dirty job of cleaning out the attic of an abandoned building. I thought they looked cool. In retrospect, they didn't, but worse than that is what would have happened had a rock shattered the lenses of those ancient goggles. As a broke young college student, when it became necessary to change my bike's worn rear tire, I bought a new tire and set out to do the job myself, unburdened by proper tools, useful experience, or good advice. I took the tire to the service station where my best friend worked (this was back when businesses that sold gasoline actually provided services beyond selling lottery tickets and six brands of energy drinks). In between my friend's transactions with paying customers, we hacked away at the task, using screwdrivers in place of the tire irons we didn't have. We mounted the tire four or five times, each time finding that we'd poked yet another hole in the old inner tube, which we were re-using to avoid further expenditure (we thought). Each time, we patched the tube. Each time, we tore it again.

Eventually, when the patched spots threatened to exceed the unpatched areas, we realized we needed both a new inner tube and professional help. Defeated, I hauled the wheel and tire to the local shop for a new tube and a professional mounting job.

Weather occasionally helped me get into trouble beyond what my poor judgment could accomplish on its own. Along with a lack of quality motorcycle training programs back in the day, we also suffered (unknowingly) from the absence of weather radar available twenty-four hours a day on the internet. Still, I should have checked the forecast before leaving for that one memorable weekend camping trip, which culminated with me returning to my camp site after dark, in the pouring rain, to find my camping gear stolen. That night may have pegged the scale for despondency, but sharper emotions followed on a much colder December night.

Having procured work for the local newspaper during my long holiday break from college, I was using my old Honda for basic transportation, despite the season, because that was all I had. In any case, I didn't have far to go on the evening in question, just a ride of a few miles across town to shoot a quick photo at a Christmas activity. Job done, photo in the camera, I walked outside into what had been a crisp but dry winter evening, only to find a thin coating of snow on my bike and more falling steadily. And it was sticking to the street.

I strapped the camera over my shoulder, grimly thinking that if I had to replace it after using it as body armor in a crash, I'd be out a week's worth of my meager wages. Maybe two weeks' worth if the boss wasn't generous in calculating the old camera's depreciation. I made it out of the parking lot, the rear tire threatening to spin with every tenderly made gear change.

I made it down the main street at 20 mph, creeping along on the slick snow, unsympathetically ignoring the drivers I was delaying behind me. I made it through a particular S-curve I'd worried about all the way home and remembered to cross the railroad tracks at a right angle, steady on the throttle, hands off the brakes. Two blocks from home, on a side street, no traffic to worry about. Just come to a nice smooth stop at the stop sign, which I did, without locking up the wheels. Yes! I'm going to make it! Exultation!

That's when I put my foot down. And it slid out from under me. And the bike fell over, taking me with it. Shards of a shattered turn signal lens skittered across the snowy street with a holiday twinkle, the clutch lever curled up in a festive imitation of a runner on Santa's sleigh, and I unleashed a holiday greeting to the empty street that was none too jolly.

But I did save the camera.

Another incident, years later, is one that occasionally still comes to mind and causes a shudder, considering what could have happened. I've heard it said that few things focus a man's mind like being told he will be executed at dawn. Let me suggest another scenario that intensely focuses a young man's mind: wind-driven gasoline streaming toward his crotch just inches from hot engine parts.

Years ago in my single days, I lived in Orlando, Florida, and would ride down to West Palm Beach many weekends to visit a young woman who lived there. I owned the original Yamaha Virago 750 with what I considered to be a stylish dark gray gas tank, nearly charcoal in color. To avoid the monotony and tolls of the Florida Turnpike, I would ride south on U.S. 441 to the town of Okeechobee and then shoot straight southeast on Florida 710. One hot and sunny Florida day, I stopped at

Okeechobee for fuel and pulled up to the pumps while paying too little attention. Pulling off my helmet in the heat, I saw an attendant with a somewhat puzzled expression walk up. It seems I had stopped at the full service pump, perhaps one of the last left in Florida. Now those of you who ride in Oregon and New Jersey know the drill, thanks to state laws that ban self-service, but the rest of us have seen nothing but self-serve pumps for many years and some probably prefer it that way. It seemed too late to change my course, though—the attendant already had the nozzle in hand—so I let him fill the tank.

Now, I could be wrong, but I imagine little happened in Okeechobee, and I'm sure the bored pump jockey hadn't seen many motorcyclists ride up to the full-service pump. His lack of experience nearly led to my demise. Having filled the tank, he decided to run up the sale amount to the nearest half dollar, just as he always did, no doubt, with cars. My little tank couldn't take it. By the time he gave up, the tank was filled to the cap, and I set off down the loneliest stretch of Florida 710 in the hot sun. Of course as that hot sun hit my stylish charcoal-colored gas tank, the cool gasoline inside began to expand. By the time I was out of town and rolling down the bowling alley-straight two-lane, gasoline was flowing freely out of the gas cap and streaming down the tank toward my crotch, where it threatened to drip onto the rear cylinder of the air-cooled V-twin engine.

Let me tell you, my mind was quite focused as I considered my equally unappealing options. The thought of stopping by that desolate roadside led to visions of even more expanding gasoline flowing out and dripping all over the hot, air-cooled engine, threatening all-out conflagration. The thought of continuing down the road led to images of becoming a rolling fireball with a freshly filled tank of fuel. If external combustion did break out, which would be worse? Abandoning the motorcycle at the first hint of ignition and tumbling down the pavement at speed, or having a fine imitation of a flame-thrower aimed at my most sensitive parts for the time it would take me to slow down and dismount?

These, my friends, are questions that have no good answers.

My focused mind quickly produced a stop-gap solution. Without slowing, I reached behind me and pulled an old shirt out of my seat bag. I wedged the crumpled shirt between my legs at the base of the tank, hoping it would soak up the gasoline and keep it from dripping onto the engine, or onto me. If flames did ignite, I didn't want to be wearing gasoline-soaked clothing. And I didn't want to stop. I kept riding down that empty highway, glancing nervously down at the tank and thinking that any minute now, any slow-moving, abnormally long minute now, I'd burn off enough fuel to outpace the thermal expansion. Never did I wish for poor fuel economy like I did that day.

Fortunately, no combustion occurred. When I arrived, the sacrificial old shirt went straight into the dumpster and after I washed off the residual gasoline smell, you wouldn't have known I'd nearly been barbecued and left for gator appetizer on one of Florida's emptiest roads. You wouldn't have known if I hadn't told you. But what's the fun of surviving our own foolishness and living to tell the tale, if you don't tell the tale? Just ask Tom McGuane.

THE MOST IMPORTANT
MOTORCYCLE EVER BUILT

*It's not exactly the stuff of dreams and doesn't
have enough power to get out of its own way,
but it's still the most important motorcycle
ever built.*

In May of 2008, Spanish racer Dani Pedrosa was leading the
MotoGP World Championship standings on his Honda RC-
212V, one of the most sophisticated two-wheeled racing machines on earth, producing more than 200 horsepower from its
800cc V-4 engine and tamed by a sophisticated electronic trac-

tion control system to limit wheelspin. That same month, at a Honda factory in Marysville, Ohio, a Honda Gold Wing, the ultimate in touring motorcycles, rolled off the assembly line with a six-cylinder engine and features ranging from a remote-control trunk opener to a satellite-linked navigation system. It even had an air bag. In fact, that Gold Wing had more individual parts than a Honda Accord car. Also that month, somewhere in the world, somebody bought a Honda Super Cub, a humble, not-worth-a-second-glance, scooter-like machine with a 50cc engine producing maybe five horsepower.

There is no doubt which of these three machines is Honda's most important.

That's because the unimposing 50cc bike sold in May of 2008 was the 60 millionth Cub series motorcycle sold in a long line that began with sales of 24,195 Super Cub C100s in Japan in 1958. Everything that has come since for Soichiro Honda's company, from global success selling cars to victorious feats of engineering in Formula One, owes a debt to that otherwise unimpressive motorcycle that, to borrow an overused phrase, is not fast enough to get out of its own way. Through its engineering advances, corporate philosophy, and racing successes, Honda has affected the motorized world many times and ways. But the significance of the Super Cub series is how it affected millions of people's personal mobility worldwide, transformed the motorcycle market in the United States—and, not irrelevant to this story—diverted my own personal history.

In 1959, Honda sent thirty-nine-year-old Kihachiro Kawashima to the United States to establish the company's foothold in the world's biggest consumer market. Despite Honda's success in Japan, there was no guarantee the company would prosper in the far different environment of the United States. More motorcycles were sold in post-war Japan, where they were seen as transportation, than in the much larger U.S. market, where they were mainly seen as toys or associated with outlaw gangs. Nobody was selling anything like the little Honda Dreams, Benlys and Super Cubs that Kawashima began promoting to dealers from the first American Honda location in Los Angeles. The Super Cub (called the Honda 50 in the U.S.) was a sharp contrast from the paint-shaker, oil-dripping, heavyweight American-made and British-built bikes of the era. Kawashima had no intention of trying to win Harley riders away from their iron-cylinder Hogs. Instead, he aimed to create a new market.

In 1963, the huge U.S. firm Grey Advertising came up with what is now the most famous slogan in the history of the U.S. motorcycle industry: "You meet the nicest people on a Honda." Not Hells Angels. Not someone wearing grease-soaked jeans and poking at his motorcycle's points along the side of the road, hoping to get it running again. Instead, magazine ads depicted housewives and families and a young couple dressed as if they were on their way to the country club on their fun little Honda 50. Although most people in the United States were probably as far from the country club lifestyle as they were from the outlaw biker stereotype, it was easier to buy into the Honda image than the Hells Angels image. For one thing, it required less money and fewer tools. Along with thousands of inexpensive and reliable Japanese motorcycles that followed in the 1960s and 1970s, the Honda 50, with its quiet four-stroke engine, step-through scooter-like styling, centrifugal clutch (you could ride it even if you didn't know how to operate a clutch) and unimposing presence offered an entirely new way to get into motorcycling. The biggest generation of U.S. motorcyclists was born.

Then there was my father.

He also bought a Honda 50, but for reasons that were 100 percent practical, utterly free of any delusions of joining the country club set, meeting nice people, or gradually working his way into hard-core, grease-stained biker society. In 1967, we moved from West Virginia, where every member of my family had been born for several generations, to Columbia, South Carolina, where my father planned to finish his master's degree at the University of South Carolina. It was just a one-year stop. For that year, my mother got a job teaching and needed to use the one and only family car to get to work. My father needed cheap transportation to get to class. As cheap as possible, since our family of four was living on one income. In 1967, "cheap as possible" meant a Honda 50. He bought one for $245 brand new and could ride about 100 commuting miles on a thirty-four-cent gallon of gas. That made it efficiently frugal transportation, as long as you didn't need to go more than 35 mph to get from where you were to where you needed to be.

My memories involving the Honda 50 during that year in South Carolina show just how much things have changed. To begin with, on the bookcase in my home office is a small black-and-white photo my mother must have taken that shows my father, my little sister, and me all posed on the Honda 50 in the front yard, in an unintentional imitation of thousands of Third World families who really did pile onto one of the little bikes and haul their goods to the town market. This difference was that we weren't going anywhere when the photo was shot, and my father's plaid Bermuda shorts certainly didn't fit the Third World theme. I recall an elementary school fundraising fair, when one family brought a pony and charged for pony rides in a circle around the school playground. My father volunteered to bring the Honda 50 and gave similar rides. Kids could choose: pony ride, scooter ride, or both. Try getting motorcycle rides covered under your parent-teacher organization's liability insurance policy these days. But the Honda 50's most unusual duty came one morning when Columbia received a rare dusting of snow and school was canceled. Now, it's not like we were from the far north, but we were still incredulous that a mere sugar frosting of the ground was enough to declare the streets unfit for schoolchildren. Also, for reasons I cannot now explain, we had packed our sled when we moved south. So there we were with a free day, a thin layer of snow that was not likely to last until noon, a perfectly flat yard, and a sled. My father put these ingredients together, tied the sled to the back of the Honda 50, and hauled us around the yard. I'm not a father, but if I were, I would be sure to do something wacky like that at least once in life, just so my children would never forget it.

The following year, we moved to Florida, my father returned to working full-time again (and driving to work in the family car) and the Honda 50 was parked. The story could have ended there, with the little bike eventually liquidated in some half-remembered manner. But just as the Honda 50 was a milestone machine for the industry, our particular Honda 50 was equally influential in my personal history. It went on to live several postscripts, long after the completion of its original one-year mission of getting my father to class in grad school.

The first postscript came that first year in South Daytona, Florida. Now a stay-at-home mom in a warm climate, my mother looked around the house after my father left for work in the car and did the expedient thing: She learned to ride the

Honda. It wasn't difficult, after all. Unlike my father, who would never ride again once he got back into his car, my mother caught the motorcycling addiction. She used the Honda 50 to take my sister the short distance to kindergarten, for errands, and for the part-time job she got working for the 1970 U.S. Census.

After a couple of years, we moved back to West Virginia and, with both my parents working full-time, the little red Honda 50 sat far more than it ran. Then it was my turn. Before I was old enough to get a driver's license, my first solo motor-cycle rides were loops out and back our unpaved driveway on the Honda 50. Learning to ride on a rutted, two-track gravel driveway lined on both sides by a barbed-wire fence enforced a certain kind of discipline that was probably a good start for a new rider.

Both my mother and I still ride, though she has moved on to slightly bigger motorcycles and I've moved on to just about everything I've ever had the chance to ride. Our original Honda 50 was eventually given to a friend of mine who turned the task of getting it in shape into a learning opportunity for a neighborhood kid without a father. Where it is today, I don't know—where it took us is what really matters to me.

For years, as our Honda 50 sat unused in a shed while I moved around the hemisphere, I rarely thought of the old bike. But when tens of millions of something are scattered around the world, reminders inevitably pop up. Thus another post-script to our Honda 50 story came many years ago when my wife and I took a short vacation to the Dominican Republic. Staying as far from the tourism resorts as possible, we traveled to Jarabacoa, a small mountain town that in earlier, pre-air conditioning times, had been a vacation spot for locals who wanted to escape the coastal heat. In the mid-1990s, when we were there, it was just a green, breezy, peaceful *pueblito* with only remnants of its past as a destination. But what surprised me about Jarabacoa was that the entire town was buzzing with Honda Super Cubs. Though newer, they looked just about identical to the one I rode as a kid on our gravel driveway in West Virginia. They served as the town's rental car fleet (my wife chose a horseback ride, instead, just as some kids did at my elementary school fundraiser in 1968). They were easily the most common form of personal transportation. They even made up the local taxi fleet. Need a lift? Hop on the back of a Cub-for-Hire and get a ride home from the store, your bags of groceries slung over your back. Jarabacoa was Scooterville. Cub City. It was a scene I would have expected, maybe, in Southeast Asia, but how did everyone in this Caribbean outpost decide to buy identical motorcycles pulled from my childhood?

Of course with 60 million sold, Super Cubs are everywhere, and the story is not yet finished. Honda still builds Cubs in fifteen countries. In Japan, the little bike even comes now with a fuel-injection system. But it still travels around 100 miles on a gallon of gasoline while sputtering out just a handful of horsepower and maybe—maybe—can hold 35 mph on an uphill grade, if the rider is skinny. In other words, it's still not exactly the stuff of dreams, still doesn't have enough power to get out of its own way, and is still the most important motorcycle ever built.

WHAT MY MOTORCYCLE
TAUGHT ME ABOUT WOMEN

*How a Harley-Davidson Sportster helped me
choose, win, and keep a wife.*

A motorcycle can be many things. In the dreams of a young boy in Italy, a motorcycle can carry him to fame and stardom at Mugello or Imola the way a boy in Texas spins a football in his hands and dreams of playing quarterback for the Dallas Cowboys. In India, a motorcycle can be basic transportation for a family of four. In London, a motorcycle may even be a specially equipped taxi to whisk you to the airport faster than a four-wheeled vehicle can negotiate the city's infamous traffic. And in the United States, a motorcycle can be, among many other things, quite an effective Rohrschach test.

I always watch closely to see the reactions of non-riders when they find out I ride, especially when they learn that it's not just a casual hobby that could be discarded any time it loses my interest, but that I ride far more than I drive a car, and that motorcycling is tied up with part of what I do for a living and is an enduring part of my identity. Their reactions often tell me a lot about their personalities, their perspectives on risk, their level of adventurousness, curiosity and open-mindedness. Then again, I have to be careful reading people's reactions, because there's an awful lot of external baggage involved. In the United States, people's perceptions of motorcycles have been molded and muddied by a chaotic soup of influences that includes bad 1960s biker movies, an uncle who owned a motorcycle for one year back in the day and still limps as a result, and the sight of swarms of middle-aged re-entry riders buying expensive cruisers with the discretionary funds siphoned from home equity lines of credit in the pre-housing-bust days. Of course if there's ever a time you really, really need to peer deep into someone's personality and glean every possible scrap of information about her attitudes toward life, it's when you're considering spending the rest of your life with her. My motorcycles helped me learn a lot about my wife to be.

The first time I took Ivonne for a motorcycle ride was quite possibly the most ill-advised two-up ride I've ever taken, and certainly not an especially enjoyable one. Fortunately for me, it was the first time she had ever been on a motorcycle so she had little basis for comparison and wasn't fully aware of what a bad idea it was. (Give her credit for intelligence, however. She suspected.) Nearby the apartment I was renting in a converted house on the outskirts of the metro sprawl of San Juan, Puerto Rico, is a little road that coils tightly for a three-mile stretch through thick forest and rarely opens up enough to allow a motorcycle to get beyond second gear. In the day, it's an idyllic ride, if you aren't in a hurry. The forest canopy easily covers and shades the narrow roadway and views through the apexes of some tight corners are blocked by thick stands of old bamboo, their tightly clustered trunks squeaking and creaking as they shift against each other with every breeze. Only a few houses are scattered along this three-mile stretch of incessant curves. Of course the lack of houses and the thick trees mean that the road is buried in utter darkness at night. No light penetrates the trees to augment the headlight's ability to illuminate potholes in the old pavement or, worse yet, the slick spots where the deep shade allows dampness to linger all day long. We once came upon police investigating a crime scene on that road. Because it is so dark, but still so close to the city, someone had found it to be a convenient place to hastily dump a bullet-filled body.

Of course, I wasn't thinking of any of those practical matters that balmy tropical evening when Ivonne was at my apartment and decided she'd like to have her first-ever motorcycle ride. I was thinking about how pleasant and shady it was on hot afternoons. It didn't take me long to realize I'd made a mistake, but turning around in the tomb-like darkness on that narrow lane seemed like a worse option than riding out those three miles before we returned to streetlights and a small community of homes. I took it slow. She kept quiet and didn't complain. And thus the first lesson I learned about my future wife, thanks to my motorcycle, was that she trusted me. Even when she shouldn't.

Fortunately, many rides followed, much more pleasant than the first. Not too long into our relationship, I found a good deal on a used Harley-Davidson Sportster. I admit that the initial attraction was mostly physical (something about the blue paint that matched the hues of the tropical skies over the ocean), but there were practical benefits, too. If you live in the Nevada desert and have to cover long distances, a Sportster is probably not your best choice of motorcycle, but it's well suited to life in a crowded urban corner of a small island: supremely narrow for lane-splitting through clogged traffic, lots of low-end torque for grunting from traffic light to traffic light, a surprisingly handy range of steering lock for squeezing through urban obstacles, and consistently good fuel mileage. And who needs long-haul capability on an island that's 100 miles long? I bought the bike without telling anyone, and I wasn't totally sure what she'd say when she saw it. I certainly didn't *need* a second motorcycle, and I was definitely planning to keep my Suzuki. Lots of women might have argued that my money would have been better spent on a first car than a second motorcycle, something a bit more appropriate for classier dates. Or maybe better spent on those classier dates at better restaurants than the ones we frequented. Or maybe better spent upgrading my minimalist wardrobe. I'm sure, in fact, that those thoughts crossed her mind, but when I surprised her by picking her up on the Sportster for a short ride to a favored but definitely un-fancy neighborhood pizzeria, she shared my excitement about the new bike rather than questioning my good sense. That's when my motorcycle helped me learn another lesson about her: that she accepted me for who I was and shared my joy, rather than trying to change me and my joys to match hers.

Now anyone who has spent any time on a Sportster knows that it's not the ideal two-up motorcycle. So I repaid her trust and acceptance by fitting the Sportster with a more comfortable seat and a low backrest to make her feel more secure. Later, she would admit that she knew I was serious about the relationship when I modified my motorcycle to make her happier. Over the next year, we took many rides on that Sportster. I was determined to see every corner of the island and truly get to know the place I was writing about. For her, a confirmed city girl, many of those outings onto country roads that got smaller and smaller the farther we ventured into the mountains were first-time trips to corners of her homeland she'd never seen. I took her to places she'd never had reason to go to, because I didn't need a reason. And she was my cultural guide, explaining to me all the beauty and meaning and complexity in what we saw. Because of those weekend motorcycle rides, I learned that despite a mother who had taught her as a girl to shun motorcycles, despite an inborn preference for high heels over boots, and despite a justifiable desire for comfort instead of hardship in a life that had already dealt her enough of the latter, she was still willing, even eager, to join me on the back of that poorly suspended, roughly vibrating Sportster for another excursion to some odd and distant spot I'd picked out on the map. I learned there was an adventurous streak beneath the polished exterior, and that was a very important lesson for this man to learn.

The most memorable motorcycle ride we took in those courting days, however, was a ride that by itself would have been less than ordinary. It was the kind of route we'd normally avoid, a four-lane toll road and some busy local roads along the north coast, the most populous area of the island. But at the end of that ride was a spot I had carefully selected, a small inn perched over a rocky bluff above the Atlantic at the edge of a town called Quebradillas. On that warm and sunny day in May, we rode there with a ring in my pocket, and rode back with the ring on her finger. Every now and then, on the return ride eastward, I'd feel her give me a little squeeze as the motorcycle carried us toward her parents' house to break the news. We felt right together on the bike, and I felt like I'd done the right thing.

During the early years of our marriage, her health wavered and there were periods of time, which seemed like long periods of time, when it was too painful for her to ride with me at all. Sometimes when I rode alone, and saw views I instantly and instinctively wanted to share, I'd reach out to pat her knee and point, but instead I'd find an empty spot behind me. The motorcycle reminded me of what was really important.

Another time, on one of those days when our outing was a bust, when every place we went to was too crowded, too hot, and too much a waste of our precious weekend afternoon, we were riding home in heavy traffic. I was frustrated, my mind was not focused. We topped a rise to find traffic ahead of us at a complete standstill because of a bad accident ahead. I don't know where my attention was focused at that moment, but in my distracted state, it wasn't on the road, where it should have been, and I reacted too late. I clipped the corner of the bumper of the car ahead before I could come to a stop and down we went in the median of the highway. Hours later, an X-ray of her hand had shown no broken bones, just bruises. That day, the unhappiest moment I've ever had on a motorcycle, the ride taught me another lesson about my wife. That she readily and easily forgave me for my errors, even when the cost could have been high.

All of those lessons came many years ago now, but there's one more postscript to this story. For our tenth wedding anniversary, I wanted to take Ivonne to one of the truly beautiful spots in the world, some place that would be memorable for both of us. On my short list of places in the United States I had yet to visit, but *had* to visit someday, was Glacier National Park in Montana. Maybe I used a little too much salesmanship, but she agreed to go. Of course there was no way I could imagine crossing the Going-to-the-Sun Road for the first time in my life and doing it in a rental car. That just wouldn't do. At the same time, I knew I'd better make plenty of accommodations for her vacation tastes and comfort level, or this wouldn't be the kind of anniversary memory I wanted to make. So I booked nights at the most charming bed and breakfast I could find in Great Falls, Montana, for the night of our arrival by plane and the night before our return flight. For transportation to and within Glacier, I rented what I personally believe is the most comfortable motorcycle yet invented, the Harley-Davidson Ultra Classic Electra Glide (and yes, I've ridden a Gold Wing, and yes, it's very close and just a matter of personal opinion). Everything went according to my carefully laid plans except the one thing that nobody can control, the weather. Instead of the average temperatures of highs in the seventies, we hit a cool spell, though fortunately no rain. We needed every bit of that Electra Glide's massive fairing, but settled into its protective envelope, we made it to the east side of Glacier without problems. All went well until the arrival of the supposed highlight of the trip, a leisurely ride on the Going-to-the-Sun Road across Logan Pass, followed by a lakeside lunch at one of Glacier's famous old lodges just oozing with Western character and history. Of course the cold snap meant that temperatures at the top of the pass were in the forties, and the walls of snow cleared off the road, which were still ten feet tall in spots, didn't help. At least psychologically, those snow banks made it feel like we were riding through a refrigerator, even if they didn't actually lower the temperature all that much. By the time I pulled into the visitors center at the top of Logan Pass, my tropics-born bride of ten years was shivering, despite wearing just about every article of clothing she'd packed. As we walked around the visitors center, trying to admire the views through the glass walls, she walked off by herself for a few moments, and when I approached I saw a few tears. That's right, she was so cold, her hands still frozen through her inadequate gloves, that she started tearing up. What made it more heartbreaking is that she even apologized for not being tough enough to enjoy the ride, since I was obviously relishing the ride through these glorious peaks.

Of course, I had warmer gloves, too.

Now that it's well into the past, that trip to Glacier makes for a funny story that never fails to bring out a few laughs as Ivonne recounts her tears at the top of Logan Pass, while around us happy families pointed at amazing distant Rocky Mountain views and nearby ground squirrels while laughing kids in T-shirts threw June snowballs at each other. And I take my lumps and laugh and admit that, yes, I made my wife cry on our tenth anniversary. Pointing out that the weather was sunny and sixty-five degrees at the bottom of the pass, where we had a great lunch at Lake McDonald Lodge, rarely seems to rehabilitate my image as much as I'd wish.

After ten years of marriage, one might think he knows

nearly everything worth knowing about his wife. But some things you may not really know for sure. Even after all that time, that motorcycle ride revealed one more truth: The woman's in it for the long haul. She'll stick with me through good and bad, even through the snowbanks of Logan Pass, where her Puerto Rican blood was never meant to go. And I know this because of a motorcycle ride.

WHAT IS IT ABOUT RACING?

Some love it, some love to ignore it. Either way, motorcycle racing brings out passions.

The rider hunches himself tighter than a jockey on a thoroughbred, his neck jerked back at an inhuman angle, his chest pressed against the metal of the gas tank, which pounds his sternum when even the slightest bump comes too hard and too fast for the taut suspension to damp it. He hears his own engine screaming between his knees, its pistons violently reversing direction dozens of times per second, but he also hears the sound of another screaming engine, another motorcycle, somewhere over his shoulder, ridden by another, equally adrenaline-powered, hyper-competitive racer, who desperately wants nothing more on earth than to be in front of him. So he holds, holds, forces himself to hold the throttle as the braking marker rushes toward him, and at the last possible moment before the only outcome imaginable is a tumbling crash, he sits up into the 190 mph wind blast to slow for the right hand corner ahead. Now comes the really hard part.

Despite the wind desperately trying to rip him off the bike, despite the speed and the acceleration and braking forces of his hurtling flight, his every move must be as precise as a surgeon's. Every part of his body goes to work, every synapse of mental processing power called into play to sense every twitch from the bike and to maximize the precision of the instructions to all those parts of the racer's body. Two fingers of his right hand squeeze the front brake lever, tensely seeking the point of maximum deceleration, which lies just this side of front wheel lockup and disaster. The left hand pulls the clutch while the left foot shifts down through the gears, and the right hand, already busy with the crucial task of braking, works the throttle to keep the revs in line with the downshifting. The legs begin shifting his weight to the right, in one fluid motion, careful not to unsettle the already strained chassis, as he prepares to hang off for the turn. The upper body strains against the wind blast over the top of the small fairing, a strain that must not be fed into the handgrips, because the front tire, already at the limit, can take no more inputs. The stresses on the front tire heat it to the melting point, the strands of rubber compound melting and reforming at a microscopic level, leaving behind the tell-tale feathering typical of a spent tire at the end of a race. With the weight of the motorcycle and rider fully shifted to the front tire, the rear tire rises off the ground slightly, skimming the asphalt, a forgotten follower for the moment, as all the action is taking place at the front. The rear of the bike moves side to side slightly, like a dog wagging its tail in super slow motion, the rider keeping the motorcycle's two wheels roughly in line with minor changes in his position and pressure on the grips, changes so minor and instinctual after years and years of riding that he doesn't think of them, they just happen. As he begins his lean in the corner, he's still trailing the front brake, but much more lightly now, as almost all the front tire's precious traction must be reserved for cornering, leaving little for braking. Hanging off the right side of the bike, knee scraping the asphalt, elbow barely flying above the raised red-and-white curb, eyes intently looking through the apex of the turn, mind already thinking beyond the demands of this second to what must come next, the crucial moment when the right hand can again twist the throttle and desperately call for enough power from the engine and enough grip from the shredding rear tire to stay ahead of the other riders on the same edge of their ability and their motorcycles' capabilities.

That's one corner of one race. String them together for an entire race, then an entire season of races, and if your ability to find that fine line between mastery and disaster is among the best in the world, you may achieve riches and glory. If you're off by a couple of seconds a lap, you may make a better living as an accountant. You'll certainly be less likely to be maimed on the job.

In case you can't tell, I love this stuff. I admire the skill, I enjoy the spectacle.

I realize not everyone does.

It's one of those things that adds to the diversity of motorcycling and sometimes also leaves me mystified. There are hundreds of thousands of avid riders in this country who have never been to a race, couldn't name one top rider, and probably couldn't even say for sure what kind of motorcycles are raced professionally. I can understand that. What a boring world it would be if we all liked the same things. The mystifying part is the visceral objection to racing I find among some riders. They've gone beyond "I don't care for it and have no interest," to "If I see one more race bike on the cover of your magazine I'm going to cancel my subscription." Meanwhile, on a summer Sunday in Italy, the top-rated program on television is likely to be a MotoGP race, and more than 100,000 people will flock to the same race in Spain. Even in our country, there are thousands of kids training and working to be the best at their local motocross track, hoping to be the next Ricky Carmichael or James Stewart. It's one of those motorcycle sub-cultures that go unnoticed by many riders, but its intensity is hard to overestimate.

Personally, I enjoy many kinds of racing, both two wheels and four. If I were an off-road rider I'd probably pay more attention to motocross or enduros. An epic like the Dakar Rally captures my attention just because of the sheer demands it places on the racers' stamina, endurance, and mental strength. But it should come as no surprise that the form I most enjoy is motorcycle roadracing. It's the closest to what I do, which is ride a street motorcycle, though once you understand the skill involved at the professional level, you come to realize it's not really all that close. That skill gap between amateurs and pros is there in any sport. The best player in the local YMCA recreational basketball league is only superficially playing the same game as an NBA player. Similarly, even a very competent street rider who works at being smooth and thinks of himself as a fast rider is a wounded slug compared to the pros. Having taken the Kevin Schwantz and Jason Pridmore riding courses, I've been on the track with several pros. As I rode near my limit, they cruised comfortably ahead of me, demonstrating proper technique and preferred lines, operating video cameras, monitoring my form in their mirrors and generally not breaking a sweat. They had several more gears they could shift into if needed, but for riding with the likes of me, they could turn off 75 percent of their skills. If more evidence is needed, do a track day sometime at one of the tracks the AMA Superbikes visit. Time your laps, and see just how far off the pace you are. It's sobering. How do you make up twenty seconds a lap? And then, consider this: Those guys are racing at the national level. They haven't made it to the top two rungs, World Superbike or MotoGP. Then there's motocross, where we're fortunate to have the national championship that attracts the world's best riders and has thus become the *de facto* world championship. I had the chance once to walk the Supercross track at Qualcomm Stadium in San Diego before the racing started. The jumps are steep enough to make walking difficult. Riding it? At speed? Fast enough to keep James Stewart in sight? Sure, right after I dunk on Lebron James and pound my way through the Colts front line to sack Peyton Manning.

Riding with real racers and comparing my laps to theirs gave me a level of insight that makes a day at the races even more fun than before. But just as I have a personal policy of never trying to encourage someone to take up motorcycling, unless the original motivation comes from them unbidden, I also refrain from trying to convert non-fans to racing. It's generally a futile endeavor, and I know because I've watched it from the outside. Most often, those who are evangelizing for their favored form of racing are probably the most frustrated motorcycle racing fans in the United States these days, fans of flat-track racing. Not that long ago, it was the top form of racing in this country. Now, it ranks third, at best. You see die-hard flat-track supporters pop up regularly on motorcycle message boards on the internet, bemoaning the lack of television coverage for their sport, wishing for better crowds, more impressive venues, bigger purses for the riders, and other things that aren't going to happen. They're sure that flat-track racing would soar again in popularity if only it were "promoted right." They argue that flat-track produces great, close racing and puts on a show like no other, with a pack of riders charging into the first turn shoulder-to-shoulder where they all pitch the bikes sideways at triple-digit speeds, slinging dirt, forever teetering on the edge between control and catastrophe. And you know what? On many points, they're right. Flat-track produces great, close racing. And you know what else? It doesn't matter, and no amount of promotion will significantly change the long-term trajectory of the sport. Whether you consider it a minor fact or a national tragedy, flat-track is not going to return to pre-eminence as the nation's top form of motorcycle racing any more than the fedora is going to come back into style among masses of middle-class men. Public tastes change and evolve, and while they often pay homage to the past, they rarely double back on themselves, and that includes motorcycle racing.

In the first half of the twentieth century, hillclimb was the most popular form of professional motorcycle racing in the United States. It was where you'd find the best riders and the biggest crowds. Tastes changed and flat-track took over the top spot. I'm sure at the time there were die-hard hillclimb fans lamenting the decline of their favored sport and dismissing flat-track as an inferior show and a lesser test of skill. They just did-n't have internet message boards to help spread their complaints, so they had to talk about it while hanging out at the local motorcycle shop. Today, hillclimb races are still a good show—nearly a century after the sport's heyday—but now it's essentially an amateur sport. Flat-track is sliding down that same trajectory. Someday, something will come along and surpass Supercross, or it will change until it's unrecognizable from today's vantage point. But meanwhile, if you want to know the near-term future of motorcycle racing in the United States just ask yourself this about the fans of that future. What would a kid of today, raised around techie gadgets and 24/7 entertainment on television and the internet, prefer? Going to a Supercross race in a massive stadium and seeing high-tech bikes soar over triples with fireworks and lasers and flamethrowers going off? Or going to an old county fairgrounds horse track and watching a bunch of heavier bikes—that look sort of like his grandfather's old motorcycle—turn left? Even if every flat-track main ended in a four-way dead heat across the finish line and every Supercross race was another James Stewart 20-second runaway, that kid's still going to want to see Supercross at Anaheim more than he wants to see flat-track at the Allen County Fairgrounds in Lima, Ohio.

It's not that I'm unsympathetic. On the contrary, I share the pain. I know the feeling of wondering why the world doesn't recognize the obvious greatness of my own personal favorites. Setting aside, for the moment, the currently fragile state of roadracing in the United States, which is the result of the worst possible timing of managerial turmoil arriving simultaneously with economic meltdown, I've often been frustrated by the huge gap in popularity between four-wheel and two-wheel racing in this country. It's not that I expect people who have never ridden a motorcycle to suddenly start attending Superbike weekends. But why do so many motorcycle riders seem to prefer car racing?

On a trip around Lake Superior in 2002, I found myself in Munising, Michigan on a Sunday evening. The hotel had a banquet room that doubled as a bar, and since there were no events going on, it was empty except for the bartender and a big-screen television, showing some random program. Fortunately, the bartender was happy to hunt down the Speed channel at my request and I was able to relax at the end of the day's ride and watch another chapter in the truly epic battle that year between Colin Edwards and Troy Bayliss for the World Superbike championship. If you saw any of that 2002 season, you know what I mean. American versus Aussie, Honda versus Ducati, a back-and-forth thrust and parry that culminated with Edwards overcoming a fifty-eight-point deficit to seal the title in the final laps of the final race of the season. As I watched that race in the empty hotel hall in July, most of the drama was still to come, but every race that season was one not to be missed.

The next morning, I joined some other riders for breakfast and one asked in casual fashion, "Anybody hear who won the race yesterday?"

I almost launched into an enthusiastic, turn-by-turn description of the Bayliss-Edwards battle, but something made me stop short. "Which race?" I asked. My fellow riders told me they were interested in who won the weekend's NASCAR race. Since I'd caught a glimpse of the results while watching the World Superbike race, I knew the answer. "Kevin Harvick," I said, a little glumly. No offense to Kevin Harvick, but even the name sounded boring when I said it, compared to the hand-to-hand duel I'd witnessed. I considered trying to tell them what they'd missed, what they continued to miss, but decided against it.

Much as I might wish that those fellow riders would prefer watching Ducati, Honda, and Yamaha Superbikes to Fords and Toyotas and Chevys that in reality all look exactly alike, I know a losing battle when I see one. I could make all kinds of rational arguments about why motorcycle roadracing is superior to NASCAR. The higher fitness level of motorcycle racers. The greater physical demands of motorcycle racing, as shown by the average age that riders retire, versus drivers who keep going sometimes into their fifties. The ability of fans to see the rider working the motorcycle, while the cars are just chunky billboards, with the drivers' skills, no matter how masterful, hidden from view inside. These are all logical arguments, and all of them are just as irrelevant as the dominant popularity of hillclimb a century ago.

When I finally boil it all down, an appreciation for racing is not something that comes from a rational argument or an array of statistics. It's a gut feeling. It is certainly increased by an informed appreciation for the skill involved, but it still comes down to the exciting flash of color as a racing motorcycle roars down a straight, the sound of controlled and harnessed explosions trailing behind, the tires struggling for grip as the rider tests the foothold at the edge of the abyss. You either get hooked or you don't. In the end, that's what it is about racing.

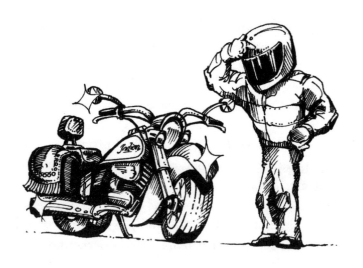

INDIAN VERSUS TRIUMPH

How Not to Revive a Famed Motorcycle Marque

Why do some rebirths succeed and others fail?
Oil leaks, exploding light bulbs, and broken
parts on a two-day ride aboard an Indian
Scout provide some clues.

A not insignificant portion of what I've learned about the motorcycle industry came from a ride across Pennsylvania on a 2001 Indian Scout that served as an excellent advertisement for Harley-Davidson motorcycles.

In 2001, to celebrate the one-hundredth anniversary of the founding of the original Indian Motocycle Co. in Springfield, Massachusetts, the resurrected Indian, then based in Gilroy, California, planned a cross-country ride from the original factory on the East Coast to the new one on the West Coast. The ride included friends of the company, factory workers who won the right to participate in a portion of the cross-country trip, and new CEO Frank O'Connell and his wife, Barbara, both avid and experienced motorcyclists themselves. It was an attractive concept. The CEO, blue-collar folks from the assembly line, loyal customers, and the occasional hanger-on invited guest (such as myself) would ride together across the United States in a symbolic journey from Indian's birth in 1901 Massachusetts to its resurrection in 2001 California.

I joined the group in Scranton, Pennsylvania, and rode with them for two days to the Motorcycle Hall of Fame Museum at the American Motorcyclist Association headquarters in Pickerington, Ohio. At the time, the museum featured an exhibit called "A Century of Indian" that marked the company's centennial, so it was a perfect stopping point for that day of the trip. Little did I know that on the museum floor, amidst a wealth of Indian history in the form of vintage motorcycles, "Indian Wrecking Crew" memorabilia from the hey-days of flat-track racing, and other artifacts of the company's past, a bit of additional history would be made.

But to get to the museum from Scranton, we first had a leisurely two-day ride across Pennsylvania and half of Ohio. The morning we were to leave Scranton, I was up early and strolled outside the hotel to examine the motorcycles before our departure. I settled into the saddles of the colorfully painted Chiefs and Scouts to see how they fit.

"I like the Chief, myself. Lets me stretch out," said one of the Indian factory workers who was along to drive the chase truck and tend to the motorcycles. He was a burly guy, easily topping six feet and somewhere well into the 200-plus range, weight-wise. When I sat on the Chief, I felt more like I was hung out to dry. The extra-wide, fully chromed handlebar spread my arms uncomfortably far apart and the gas tank loomed large between my knees. The Chief felt like a cartoonist's version of a big cruiser. The size, the chrome, the bright paint were all slightly exaggerated for effect. I've ridden enough Harley-Davidson Road Kings, Springer Softails and the like to know that the Milwaukee company has perfected the art of making a traditionally styled cruiser look big without making me feel like a jockey on its back. Unlike the Indian mechanic, I quickly decided I'd be mostly riding a Scout. But I would also soon learn that looks were not the only issue with the new Indians.

The day was sunny and pleasant, a perfect summer riding day, but the group had endured steady rain the previous day. The Indian mechanics were busy polishing dried road spray off the expansive chrome, but they had more to do than that. I noticed they were changing taillight bulbs in all the motorcycles, and with a quick look it was easy to see why. The design of the taillight lenses allowed rain water to enter, but not escape, so the red plastic lenses filled with water like little fish bowls. The hot bulbs cracked and exploded when the water level rose to touch them. Maybe Indian owners didn't plan to ride in the rain, but if they did, they'd soon be riding without tail or brake lights just when they needed them most, in poor visibility conditions, and they would also need to have a supply of bulbs on hand for day-after maintenance.

That was just my first hint that all was not perfection in Indian country. Long before we were across Pennsylvania, the speedometer failed on the Scout I was riding. All the bikes had hot oil streaming from the air cleaners, a situation that was considered normal. (And yes, I know about crankcase venting and I know Harleys do it too, but the situation seemed worse on the S&S engines used in the Indians.) The dual gas tanks on the Chiefs may have provided a historically correct appearance, but unless the owner knew and followed the correct drill for filling them, gasoline would overflow one side before the other was full, dangerously spilling onto hot engine parts and making each fill-up a potential conflagration. All this on motorcycles that cost around $20,000 in 2001 and were, to put it bluntly, little more than a set of stylized fenders on an assemblage of parts from the huge catalogs of the Harley-Davidson-based aftermarket. A few die-hard Indian fans might buy one (though an equal number were put off by the revived brand, because it wasn't a "real" 1953 Chief), but I couldn't help but conclude from my two-day ride that the product was neither good enough nor affordable enough to appeal to a broad market.

Not that O'Connell was ignorant of those facts. Those first Indians, based on parts designed for Harley Evolution engines, were always intended to be a bridge, something to sell while the company developed its own proprietary engine and other parts. On the surface, O'Connell seemed the perfect choice to lead Indian to a higher level. He was considered something of a corporate turnaround artist, having led the money-losing greeting card company, Gibson Greetings, to a profitable sale to a larger rival. He had also been an executive at Reebok Brands North America and HBO Video, among other companies. But O'Connell was more than just a business executive with a track record that could get him in the door to see the venture capitalists whose money Indian needed. He also understood motorcycles, because he had been riding them his whole life.

It was hard not to like the O'Connells. Both were skilled and enthusiastic riders and seemed like the kind of people who were comfortable in leather or Gore-Tex or the formal wear of a CEO's business world. Over dinner at the end of the day, they fondly recalled the days when they were young and living on the West Coast and would take off for two-up rides into Mexico on the cheap and non-descript Japanese motorcycle they owned at the time. Both spoke eloquently about their mission to revive Indian in a way that convinced me it was more to them than just another business, like athletic shoes or greeting cards. How, Frank mused, could you put a dollar value on the fondness for the Indian brand that still survived, fifty years after the original company stopped building Chiefs and Scouts? Could any amount of advertising ever buy you that much good will? Barbara spoke just as eloquently about the history of the company and the subtle differences in public perception of the Indian and Harley-Davidson brands. There was romance in the Indian name, she said.

Good will and romance don't meet payroll, however, and at the very moment Indian was celebrating its centennial, Frank O'Connell was preoccupied with finding the money the company needed to move ahead. As it turned out, the second of my two days with the cross-country ride was a crucial moment. As the rest of the group toured the exhibit at the Motorcycle Hall of Fame Museum, Frank was on his cell phone and borrowing use of an AMA fax machine to hammer out the final details of a $45 million injection of venture capital money that would allow Indian to build its own proprietary engine and stop relying on that initial strategy of slapping Indian-styled fenders on a collection of aftermarket Harley-Davidson parts.

Later, when I sat down to write my article about Indian, it was undeniable that the company was poised at a turning point. The crude, overpriced Scout and Chief models I had ridden had gotten the company started and had given dealers something to put on showroom floors, but they were neither the future nor even a sustainable present. Even O'Connell admitted that building the new engine and creating a "real" Indian was a make-or-break prospect for the company.

"We've got the money," he said of the new venture capital financing. "We've got the time. We must do this right."

Unfortunately, the press releases that came out of Gilroy, California, over the following months and years said more about the assemblage of an ever-growing management team than the assemblage of competitive motorcycles. When it debuted, the new 100-cubic-inch Powerplus engine suffered from assembly issues and it wasn't unique enough in the present or evocative enough of Indian's past to attract the attention the company had expected. Less than four years after that day at the museum, Indian had burned through the $45 million in venture capital money, with too much of it spent on vice presidents' salaries and not enough spent on fixing the flaws of the Powerplus engine. The new Indian followed the old Indian into bankruptcy and nearly 400 people lost their jobs. The second version of Indian joined the other unsuccessful revivals of the era, alongside the interesting Nortons built by Kenny Dreer, which fell just short of making it to mass production before the money ran out, and the efforts by the Hanlon brothers in Minnesota to revive the Excelsior-Henderson brand, which left behind hard feelings, lawsuits, losses for banks and taxpayers, worthless stock certificates, and an attractive factory built to produce 20,000 motorcycles a year, but only about 2,000 actual motorcycles. More recently, the folks who bought the dregs of Indian have begun building yet another version of the

Chief. But now, with even mighty Harley-Davidson drastically reducing production, laying off workers, and shutting down the Buell line, the fervor for resurrected historic American motorcycle marques has abated and I have to believe the most important chapters in the Indian story have already been written.

I'm not a big nostalgia fan, so an Indian was never likely to find a spot in my garage. But I do own two Triumphs, and therein lies an instructive comparison. Triumph was founded in 1902, just a year after Indian. Like Indian, it went out of business in the second half of the twentieth century, when it failed to keep up with the competition. Like Indian, it died, despite its flaws, with a huge reservoir of public affection.

When self-made millionaire John Bloor bought the remains of Triumph, he took some steps that were similar to the early days of the revived Indian, but he also followed a different approach in critical ways. Those first 1990s bikes built by the resurrected Triumph were by no means ground-breaking motorcycles. But unlike the Harley-clone Indians, they were good enough to stand on their own merits and sell for reasons other than fondness for the name on the tank. They allowed the company to get started and from there it grew into a real manufacturing firm based on modern facilities turning out products that competed on their merits. Only after the new Triumph firmly established itself with modern motorcycles did it tap into nostalgia by building the "new Bonneville." Bloor is by all accounts a clear-eyed businessman who will spend sobering sums of money on what's important but hates wasting it on what isn't. And because it is not dependent on outside financing as Indian was, Triumph was able to stay the course even when disaster hit and a fire destroyed part of the factory.

Old-timers may still talk fondly of the days when the battles were Harley versus Indian, or later, Harley versus Triumph, and took place on county fair dirt tracks. In a twenty-first-century global economy, what happens on a Midwest dirt track is as irrelevant as horseshoes to the space shuttle. I only have to look into my garage and recall the exploding taillight bulbs to know who has an insurmountable lead in the modern-day version of Indian versus Triumph.

BONDING

Some motorcycles are passing acquaintances,
scarcely remembered. Some stay with us for
life, whether in our garages or in our hearts.
What's the difference?

Several years back, a photographer friend of mine had to take a
portrait of me. Essentially, his assignment was to depict me in a
motorcycling context. The idea came to him instantly: "I'll get
a real tight shot of you with the headlights of your Speed Triple." After a short session, he had the photo he wanted, a pic-
ture of my face with an uncharacteristically broad smile,
poised next to those twin headlights that began being labeled
predictably as "bug-eye" headlights as soon as Triumph
launched the second-generation Speed Triple in 1997.

My point is not to introduce another useless dissection of

the artistic merits of the Speed Triple (Whenever anyone comments on the odd appearance of my motorcycle, I say, "Everyone loves the way it looks. Except those who hate the way it looks.") or, worse yet, bore you by delving into the psychological reasons why my smiles tend to be thin and wry rather than wide and toothy. The point is that after knowing me and riding regularly with me for a few years, he immediately seized on the most characteristic feature of that particular motorcycle to squeeze into the image, alongside my face, as a way of representing my personality in motorcycling terms. And he came to that instant conclusion because, to him, that motorcycle was damn near a part of me. For lack of a better word, he knew that I'd bonded with that bike.

Why is that?

Some of us never bond at all, but instead run through a series of short-term flings. In jocular discussions on internet message boards theses folks are referred to, often by themselves, as "bike whores." Never settling down, always looking for a new experience, always imagining that the next bike will be better. And for a while, it is. Because the newness itself, the differentness, is a big part of the allure for these riders. It can make motorcycling very expensive, if you do it the easy way. Some riders buy a new one every year, then trade it in the following season for the current "motorcycle of the year" contender (my Speed Triple was originally owned by one such rider). They take the maximum hit on depreciation and no doubt spend thousands more on motorcycling than I do. On the other hand, if you're a savvy buyer and seller and you do your own repairs and maintenance, you can almost ride for free by buying used and trading judiciously.

At the other extreme are riders who bond with one motorcycle and stick with it like an old friend, a beloved spouse, and a favored child, all rolled into one. Consider the extreme bonding, for example, of Wisconsin State Senator Dave Zien and his 1991 Harley-Davidson FXRT, which he rode a million miles before it went on display at the Sturgis Motorcycle Museum (Harley-Davidson gave him a 2009 Road Glide as a replacement to ease the pain of separation). Or there's the late Fred Tausch Jr. and his 1970 BMW R60/5, which he had ridden more than 600,000 miles when I interviewed him a few years before his death for an article about people who put big miles on their motorcycles. He saw no need to buy a new one, since the old BMW was still running. There's no doubt Ed Culberson (author of *Obsessions Die Hard*) bonded with "Amigo," his BMW R80G/S, which he rode the entire length of the Pan-American Highway, including the portion that has never been built, by dragging, winching, tugging, wrestling, and floating the poor bike through the jungle of the Darien Gap in Panama and Colombia. These are men, we can safely say, who bonded with their motorcycles.

There's a lot less drama involved in my bonding with the Speed Triple. Every time I buy a motorcycle, I expect to keep it for the long haul, but it usually doesn't work out that way. With the Speed Triple, it did, but the bonding process was a gradual one that didn't always have an air of inevitability about it. I bought the bike when it was a year old and had about 6,000 miles on it, expecting it to be a good, all-around motorcycle: practical enough for daily transportation, comfortable enough to strap on some luggage and take a trip, and fast and nimble enough to satisfy my occasional urge for a sporty ride. It wasn't perfect at any of those things, but it was competent at all of them. Over the years, I moved it, stored it, flogged it hard at times, and let it sit for other long periods of time, even took it to the track once, but I never seriously considered parting with it. It stayed with me even as other motorcycles came and went. And now, as I write this, it's thirteen years old, shows the scars and stains and scuffs from years of use, and the mileage is above 83,000. Selling it now is out of the question simply because nobody would buy it. Certainly, nobody would ever pay me anything approaching what it's worth to me for personal reasons. I keep thinking it deserves a good polishing and a subsequent easy life of semi-retirement after all it has been through, but despite a few odd electrical glitches and extra rattles and a little inevitable looseness around the bearings here and there (kind of like its middle-aged owner), it still works just fine, so I keep riding it.

I'm not the kind to name my motorcycles, or think of them as living creatures, but I do recognize the parallels between the way we bond with our bikes and the way we bond with the people in our lives. Attraction may not always start with lust, but it commonly does. I admit I have lusted in my heart for a Ducati 848, for example, but I'm certain I'll never own one. Riding one is the motorcycling equivalent of dating a model. She's undeniably beautiful, but the maintenance levels are too high and too costly and she's just a little too thin, a little too bony beneath the surface. And the fun is tempered by the nagging doubt that my performance may not live up to hers. Even when lust is not the primary driver of the initial attraction, subjective feelings remain powerful. That's why so much effort goes into styling motorcycles, even sportbikes that supposedly live and die by performance alone. Bikes such as the 1994 Ducati 916 and the 1998 Yamaha R1 broke ground in performance terms, but it was the added appeal of their good looks that sealed their places as milestone machines. In the cruiser world, fuhged-daboutit. Style and image are damn near everything.

Of course, lust and style are no deeper than a shiny paint job. To get beyond that initial attraction, you have to get to know someone. Or something. In this case, a two-wheeled something. You learn to appreciate its positive attributes and live with its drawbacks. Over the years, after you've come to know the motorcycle thoroughly and have relied on it thousands of times, it may come to feel like an old friend, one you're willing to forgive when it does let you down because so many times before it didn't.

The ideal lifelong relationship, with a human partner or a motorcycle, involves a little of all of that. It starts with a spark of lust that soon deepens into love and then ages finely over the years into the best and most lasting friendship you've ever had, at which point there's no longer any question of calling it off. You're in it for the long haul, for better or worse. Congratulations, you've bonded. You may now kiss your ride.

If it's sometimes hard to explain why we bond with some motorcycles, for me it's even more difficult to explain why I fail to bond with others. I've tried to uncover the explanations by using a classic personal case study, a motorcycle I had every reason to bond with, but didn't. The motorcycle in question was a 1997 BMW F650, a bike that has a huge worldwide following, as demonstrated by perhaps the best and most comprehensive single-model online community of owners. I had reasons, both theoretical and practical, why it should have been the sort of motorcycle I bought, bonded with, and kept for life. To begin with, I'd always wanted, but had never owned, a big single. In theory, I admired the simplicity of a single-cylinder engine and imagined how sweet it would be to combine that simplicity with enough power and comfort to be practical. When I actually found the bike I would buy, it offered plenty of practical reasons for me to bond with it, too. The BMW belonged to a friend of a friend who had been trying to sell it for months. It was fully outfitted with hard saddlebags, heated grips and an extra-large, aftermarket gas tank. My friend vouched for the obsessive level of maintenance by the owner, who happened to be a helicopter mechanic by trade. The reason he hadn't been able to sell it, despite an attractive asking price of $2,000, was the mileage: 40,000 miles. That's a lot for a single, but considering the level of maintenance, the big box of spare parts that came with the deal and the reputation of the Rotax-built engine BMW put into the F650, I jumped at it with very little hesitation. Finally, I owned a motorcycle with locking luggage and heated grips, a long-overdue development that had always been delayed by purchases of less-practical motorcycles that appealed on other levels.

Then came the final and perhaps most compelling reason to bond with the BMW. You see, one of the main reasons I bought it was to take it on a trip to Mexico. The F650 was ideal for the task. It was comfortable enough for hours on U.S. interstates to get me to the border, but capable of handling unpaved Mexican back roads in the rain, as I would find out the hard way. The BMW performed well on the trip. We should have bonded. We should have been a team for life after sharing the joys of sunny *cuotas* and the challenges of muddy detours. The bike proved to be sure-footed on slick cobblestone streets of little villages and kept my hands warm while rolling through a ferocious cold front that dipped south of the border. But well before I was home, I knew that was not destined to be. Before the month ended, the BMW belonged to someone else.

So what went wrong? Why did the BMW become a tool, bought for a specific purpose and passed along afterwards to a new owner, even though it did its intended job well, while the Triumph has become an old friend, my *compañero* in all kinds of rides, year after year, whether it accomplishes them especially well or merely adequately? I could come up with a list of semi-logical reasons, but the only one that rings true is my own unrealistic expectations. I came home from Mexico convinced that few other motorcycles can do as many things as well as my old F650, but despite that I also came home already thinking of what I'd buy to replace it. Any way I look at it, I have to conclude that the lack of bonding had more to do with the man than the machine. And I also have to conclude that some things just can't be explained satisfactorily with facts alone. Nobody *has* to ride a motorcycle, goes the old saying. It's a choice. And I'd add that almost nobody who does ride *has* to ride one particular motorcycle. It's another choice, and a very personal one, at that. Aside from falling in love, there may be few choices we make that are explained less well by facts and figures and rational calculations.

That won't stop me from continuing my quest to understand this murky business of why we bond with this bike and not with that one. Have you bonded with a bike and had the "aha!" moment when it all became clear and you understood why it happened? Or have you uncovered the reasons why certain bonds never took hold? If you have it all figured out, stop me on the road some time and explain it all to me. You'll be able to recognize me. I'll probably still be riding an old, scarred, scuffed-up Triumph Speed Triple. You know, the one with the bug-eye headlights.

RISK

*If you ever see a police mug shot of me, it
will probably be because I snapped right after
someone said, "Don't you know those things
are dangerous?"*

When I was in junior high school, there was a star athlete several grades ahead of me who set state records in baseball and was a first-string running back on the football team. I would sometimes see him running home in the dark after a long football practice to lengthen his workout, while his teammates piled into cars.

While in college, he was in a horrible car accident that left him partially paralyzed. His athletic career ended. He later bought a van and had it equipped so he could continue to drive despite his disabilities. One night he crashed into a stream in his modified van and died. Two cars had, in tragic steps, reduced a strong and graceful young man into an injured man, then a dead man.

So that's why I've never driven a car since. Clearly, those things are dangerous.

Okay, all that was a true story up until those last two lines. But you already knew that because my conclusion was absurd, right? Yet if you've been riding motorcycles for any length of time (or maybe if you've merely talked with friends or family about wanting to ride) you've probably had someone tell you a story just like that.

"My cousin's boyfriend killed himself on a motorcycle. I'd never ride one of those things."

"My father is a doctor. He calls them 'murdercycles.'"

And most annoying of all: "Don't you know those things are dangerous?"

Whenever I hear that last question, I'm tempted to exclaim, "Really? The salesman who sold me my motorcycle swore they were perfectly safe!" Then, clasping the questioner's hand and mustering utter sincerity in my eyes and voice, I'd add, "Thank you so much. I had no idea. You've probably saved my life."

I could be wrong, but I suspect that even an unobservant, shallow-thinking, carefree motorcyclist, if he or she has ridden at least 5,000 miles on the roads of the United States, knows far more about the true nature of risk than any of the confirmed car drivers who swore off motorcycles before they ever sat on one. Even if you're not really paying attention, and you're surviving more by luck than by wits, you'll see a lot of strange and dangerous antics on the road. If you're riding a motorcycle you can't help but be aware of how much higher the stakes are for you than for those better-protected drivers swerving all around you while they apply makeup, shave, make phone calls, send text messages, or aim parenting skills through the rear-view mirror at the tantrum-tossing two-year-old in the back seat.

That's why the "Don't you know those things are dangerous?" question is the most annoying of all. Of course I know
they're dangerous, or at least I know they can be. I also know
how they can be made more dangerous and I have learned and
practiced a variety of strategies for minimizing the danger. I
know how to spot and protect myself from the people on the
road (probably like my questioner) who increase the danger
quotient. I have a closet full of riding gear to protect me and an
extensive understanding of which pieces are more crucial under certain riding conditions. In short, I've spent far more time
thinking far more deeply about the true nature of risk, as well
as how to manage it, than the person who asks the question
and seems to assume that the presence of risk never even
entered my dim brain.

One of the problems for motorcyclists is the very founda-
tional philosophy of the transportation system in this country.
The underlying assumption is that crashes are inevitable, not
avoidable. That's why we call them "accidents." We're often re-
luctant to assign blame, and even slower to accept responsibility. "Accidents happen" is a common saying. "It's a tragedy," we
say in the wake of those "accidents" when someone is killed or
maimed, but less often do we say the more specific truth, that
"someone messed up" or there wouldn't have been a tragic
outcome.

Because of the attitude that crashes are inevitable, our
transportation regulations, law enforcement and infrastructure are aimed more at mitigating their destructiveness than
preventing them from happening. Thus our laws mandate
airbags in cars rather than rigorous driver education. On a divided highway with a 55 mph speed limit, you're more likely to
get a ticket for going 60 mph than for driving 50 mph in the left

lane despite all those "Slower Traffic Keep Right" signs and your disruptive effect on safe traffic flow. Because crashes are seen as inevitable, the cars with the highest "safety ratings" are those that are best equipped to withstand crashes (like a big SUV) rather than the ones most likely to avoid a crash (such as a lighter, better-handling, faster-braking car). In the hands of an inexperienced and potentially distracted teen driver out with his buddies at night, the cars we rate as "safest" don't contribute most to overall safety on the highways.

Obviously, a transportation philosophy that focuses on mitigating inevitable crashes instead of preventing them is one that doesn't favor motorcycles. Thus there's a greater burden on motorcyclists not only to take steps to minimize the consequences of a crash, but also to identify, manage, and avoid the risks that can lead to one. Of course to do that, we have to understand risk. Not everybody does.

Plenty of statisticians have pointed out that we modern humans aren't that great at accurately calculating risk. Thus, we worry more about dying in a plane crash than we do about slipping and falling in the bathtub, regardless of the true odds. But beyond that, we have to understand the nature of risk. A person whose distant relative died in a motorcycle crash and is now aghast to learn I ride is often under the misconception that what he or she does is not dangerous and what I do is. But risk is not a true-or-false question, it is a spectrum. Say you're expected to go to your aunt's house 100 miles away for Thanksgiving dinner. The spectrum lies before you. At one extreme, you could decline, stay home with the doors locked, drink filtered water and reduce your risk to perhaps as close to zero as possible. With a little risk tolerance, you could take a bus, assuming one goes to your aunt's house. With a little more, you could drive a car. Accept a bit more and you could ride a motorcycle. Add yet more risk and you could ride a bicycle, if you're fit enough. If you're a psychopathic adrenaline junkie seeking to maximize danger, I suppose you could carjack someone at the stoplight, maybe knock off a liquor store on the way and lead the police on a high-speed chase toward your aunt's house while swigging from a stolen bottle of Jack Daniels. My point is that it's a fallacy to say that driving a car is the "safe" choice and riding a motorcycle is the "risky" choice. They're both just points on the spectrum, and not really that far apart.

What it really comes down to is that each person tends to believe that the level of risk that he or she is comfortable with is an acceptable level and any additional risk (usually taken by others) is too much. Of course that's an egocentric view of the world, but unfortunately, it's the kind of limited, self-focused thinking we humans tend to fall back on when we don't consider things very deeply. Not surprisingly we have the same kind of thinking within the motorcycling world. Visit the right message boards on the internet and the second best way to start a flame war (aside from asking "What oil should I use and how should I break in my new motorcycle?") is to defend or attack the concept of ATGATT. The acronym is short for All The Gear, All The Time. At one extreme you have the ATGATT absolutists who believe that yes, you really do need to put on full leathers to ride five blocks from your house to the convenience store to buy a quart of milk for your six-year-old's Cheerios. At the other extreme are riders who want to ride helmetless and in a sleeveless T-shirt because that's the way they like it and they're willing to take the chance and they don't want anyone telling them what to do.

To me, all of this, from the philosophy that crashes are inevitable to the debates over how much risk is too much, is one gloriously elaborate waste of time. A far better use of all that energy and intellect would be for each of us, especially those of us who ride, to focus on managing our own risk. Yes, I know there's risk in riding. I just try to manage and control it so that it's commensurate with the rewards, which in my personal case are many and great. My primary strategy for managing risk is improving my own skills. Toward that end, I've completed several riding schools over the years, from the Kevin Schwantz School, which focuses purely on racetrack technique, to two Stayin' Safe Advanced Rider Training tours, which take place on the road and focus intensely on identifying and negotiating hazards on the street. Since those opportunities are limited, in between I try to read up on what smart people are saying about riding better and more safely.

I'm also a committed believer in good gear, for comfort as well as safety, even though I fall short of the standards of perfection demanded by the most ardent ATGATTistas. I have, however, put a good deal of thought behind each of my gear choices. First, I always wear a helmet for even the shortest ride, based on the logic that my brain is fragile and without it I am little more than a vegetable. Second, I always wear gloves, because my hands are also fragile and without functioning hands, I'd be pretty helpless. Not to get too graphic, but there are certain daily necessary tasks I prefer to do myself which I can't accomplish if my hands are in casts. Third, I virtually always wear some kind of jacket, because there are joints and vital organs I'd like to protect. There may be occasions, on a very short and local ride, when I won't put one on, but I can't remember the last time that happened. With today's mesh jackets, even the hottest day isn't too hot to wear one. They're nearly as cool as no jacket at all when you're moving, and along with protecting you in a crash, they also prevent sunburn. Boots and riding pants with armor are next on the priority scale. I have boots with armor and some without, and choose according to the ride. On a longer or faster ride, I often wear riding pants with knee armor, but if I'm riding three miles into town on a warm day to the hardware store? Probably not. On the track, I wear full one-piece leathers. On the street, usually textiles. All of this has a risk-reward analysis behind it that adds up to a personal level of risk acceptance, but much of it won't meet the standards of the hard-core ATGATTistas. For example, I usually wear a full-face helmet, but sometimes for short errands around town, I prefer an open-face helmet, and yes, I'm aware that if I crash face-down my wife is going to have to learn to love me for reasons other than my looks. Some scoff at my mesh jacket, saying it's insufficient for the task. And then there's my willingness to go out on the bike sometimes in jeans, not armored leather or textile riding pants. I admit that I don't meet everyone's standards of risk mitigation. Just my own.

Beyond honing one's skills and dressing for the ride, a less obvious but equally important element in managing risk is the rider's mental attitude. When I first took the Stayin' Safe course taught by my late friend Larry Grodsky, I learned the three-part mantra that was the core of his teaching: one, maintain 360-degree awareness; two, put the bike where they can't touch you (by choosing the optimum lane position based on the circumstances at any given moment); and three, no surprises. Elaborating on that third point, which was really the desired result of the first two, Larry told us that all motorcycle crashes could be avoided. "If you're aware of everything around you and you put the motorcycle in the optimum spot, you'll have no surprises, so you can avoid any crash," he asserted.

Afterwards, I went home and spent a lot of time thinking about that concept before I wrote my article about the course. In the end, I came to two conclusions. First, while the vast majority of crashes involving motorcycles could have been prevented by a rider who was more skilled or more aware, you *can't* really avoid *all* crashes. You can be riding down a two-lane road in the optimum lane position when the front left tire on an oncoming car, just thirty yards ahead of you, blows out and jerks the car into your path, both of you traveling 60 mph with a fraction of a second to react. You can (as happened to one guy I met) be riding down a multilane highway when an overhead high-tension electric line snaps and falls into your path, nearly decapitating you. My second conclusion was that although what Larry said was not 100 percent true, it was still the best way to live your life, ride your ride, and most of all, to look at it from Larry's point of view, it was the best way to teach fellow motorcyclists how to ride better. (Larry was a smart guy, even if he disguised it under a humble exterior, and he put a tremendous amount of thought and effort into being a great teacher.)

Riding and living as if you can prevent any crash from happening is the best attitude for survival because it emphasizes your responsibility for your own safety. If you adopt the prevailing view of broader society, that "accidents" are inevitable, then you have a built-in excuse to let yourself get sloppy, to work less on honing and maintaining your riding skills and to focus less intently on predicting and spotting the threats on the road. Similarly, if you believe that it's all up to fate, that if "it's your time to go" then there's nothing you can do about it, then even the most minimal risk management seems irrelevant. On the other hand, if you adopt Larry's thinking, that your fate is in your own hands, how can you justify not working to make yourself a better and safer rider? If it's up to you to determine whether your day ends as you park your motorcycle in your garage with a smile on your face or lie on an operating table in the hospital, how can you not make the effort to concentrate, to scan, to anticipate threats and avoid them?

As was proven in 2006 on a lonely West Texas road at dusk, when a deer burst into his path, Larry was, technically, incorrect. You can't avoid all motorcycle crashes, and on some level he knew that. He'd predicted to his long-time partner, Mary Ann, that a deer strike was the most likely way he'd leave this world prematurely. But even if he was technically wrong, he was absolutely right in his attitude. Sometimes, believing in something is the right thing to do, even if you can't believe that it's literally, completely, provably true all the time. Believing you can avoid all crashes is the right mental strategy for improving the odds that you will avoid them.

If some day my risk management efforts fail and my skills fall short and I suffer the same fate as Larry, don't say, "It was his time to go" and believe it was inevitable. Instead, say, "He was enjoying life's ride and he rode it as best he could," and I'll thank you from beyond.

And whatever you do, please don't say, "See? Those things are dangerous. I'd never ride one."

GHOSTS OF
MOTORCYCLING FUTURE

Consider these two news reports from alternate futures:

PARK CITY, UTAH – Summit County Sheriff's Deputies confiscated two off-road motorcycles and charged their owners with violating the Security, Energy & Efficiency Act (SEE-Act) recently passed by Congress, which outlaws the use of gasoline for most purposes other than military patrols, public safety functions, approved business activities or essential personal transportation. The arrests were the first in the nation under the new law.

"In this time of spot shortages and volatile prices, riding around in circles in the woods is not just wasteful, it threatens our national security," the U.S. Department of Energy said in a written statement. "The gasoline burned by these individuals should be used for a legitimate purpose, such as an ambulance rushing someone's child to the hospital, or a farmer bringing his crop to market, or for tanks protecting our soldiers in the Middle East."

Or:

SAN FRANCISCO – Forty square blocks in popular and busy sections of the city have been declared off-limits to gas guzzlers, but free parking is available for all electric vehicles and motorcycles and scooters that have earned the EPA's "E" designation because of their good fuel mileage.

"The federal government has done its part with tax incentives and now it's time for cities such as San Francisco to do our part," said the mayor. "These fuel-efficient vehicles help us ease the transition to new sources of energy as the price of oil becomes ever more volatile and expensive, so that's something we plan to encourage with free parking, coupled with a ban on gas guzzlers in these areas."

Two versions of motorcycling's future. Both possible. The differences depend on the perceptions of motorcycles, either as part of the problem or part of the solution. And that problem, in either scenario, is an inevitable geologic situation that's generally called "peak oil" and will be the single biggest influence on what motorcycling looks like in the future.

The phenomenon of peak oil is the subject of both too much misinformation and too little understanding, yet it will bring dramatic changes to our world. For thoseof us born in the United States in the middle third of the twentieth century, what we think of as "normal" will someday be seen as a fleeting moment in the long sweep of human history, when the world was powered by a cheap but finite supply of oil. The transition to other forms of energy will almost certainly be difficult, costly and chaotic. "The problem of the peaking of world conventional oil production is unlike any yet faced by modern industrial society." So reads a report commissioned by the U.S. Department of Energy and produced in 2005 by a research team led by Robert L. Hirsch. Whether this unprecedented challenge spawns a burst of creativity and innovation or a period of awful global conflict remains to be seen.

Simply put, "peak oil" is the moment in time when the worldwide production of oil hits its highest point and begins to decline. So what's the big deal? We'll just pay higher gasoline prices for a while until new alternatives get up to speed, right? Unfortunately, it's not likely to be that simple. To illustrate the problem, draw a straight line, rising from left to right; that's worldwide demand for oil. Then draw a bell curve over top of that line; that's worldwide production. The problem arises on the right side of the graph—our future—where supply and demand grow ever further apart with each day that passes. Of course, that's an oversimplification, because demand growth is not a perfectly straight line and production is not a smooth bell curve, but reality is not much different from my homemade graph. The crucial piece of information that we don't know, and can't know for sure, is exactly where we are on that chart. We can't recognize the peak until we pass it. Some geologists believe global oil production is hitting its peak right now. Others say it is still too far into the future to pinpoint. In 2010, the United States military, perhaps the single largest user of petroleum in the world, expressed concern that it could happen by 2015. Only with hindsight will we know for sure who is right.

The fact that it is impossible to predict is what will make it so disruptive. In his report, Hirsch estimated that if a crash course of mitigation efforts was begun twenty years before the peak, shortages could be avoided. Unfortunately, since we don't know when it will happen (or if it has already), it's likely we won't act at all until the crisis is clearly upon us, a course which Hirsch projects will lead to twenty years of disruptions.

That could take the form of volatile spikes in prices, localized food shortages (because of modern farming's heavy reliance on petroleum products and transportation), global recession, and even wars fought over resources.

Can all that be avoided? Let's look at a few simple numbers that crystallize the situation. The world currently consumes about 85 million barrels of oil per day. The International Energy Agency (IEA) projects that worldwide energy use will grow 1.5 percent annually and demand for oil will reach 107 million barrels per day in 2030. To meet that level of demand, every oil-producing country on earth would have to maintain its current level of production (some major producers, such as Mexico, are already declining quickly) and we would have to add new sources equal to double Saudi Arabia's daily output. If you're not convinced there will be any shortages, price spikes, or other disruptions, you have to ask yourself this question: Where are we going to find two more Saudi Arabias in the next twenty years?

That's the supply side of the equation. What about demand? Will it really rise, as the IEA projects? Didn't a bunch of people trade in their thirsty SUVs in the "cash for clunkers" program? Didn't gasoline use decline in the United States due to the recession? Yes, but the oil story is no longer centered on the United States. The IEA predicts that use of liquid fuels in Western Europe, the United States, and Japan will remain flat, thanks to greater vehicle efficiency and the use of alternative energy sources, but worldwide consumption will grow. Of the 22-million-barrel-per-day difference between 2006 and 2030, the IEA expects China alone to account for 8.1 million barrels per day. By 2021, Asia will use more oil than North America.

This shift is powered by millions of people joining the middle class in China, and to a significant but lesser degree in India, Brazil and other developing countries. Consider this: There are about 750 gasoline-powered vehicles per thousand people in the United States and about four per thousand in China. The Chinese have a long way to go to catch up, but they're working on it. In 2006, auto sales in China surpassed Japan and they surpassed U.S. sales for at least one month in 2009. Suddenly, it's obvious why China—limited in fossil fuel reserves, but flush with U.S. dollars—is buying up energy sources around the world. Someone's going to have to provide gasoline for all those cars.

Some skeptics of peak oil's impact dismiss the concerns and offer reassuring statistics: "We're not running out of oil. There's enough oil in U.S. waters in the Gulf of Mexico to meet the United States' needs for ten years." Or, "Brazil just found eight billion barrels of the stuff." Or, "Canada has greater oil reserves than any country in the world except Saudi Arabia." These statistics are true, but they miss the real significance of peak oil.

Yes, the recently discovered Tupi field off the coast of Brazil is immense. But getting to that crude means getting a drill through 7,000 feet of water, 10,000 feet of sand and rocks, and a 6,600-foot layer of salt, from a platform nearly 200 miles from shore. As much as we might long for the good old days of 1998 (when oil was cheapest in history, price adjusted for inflation), we won't be able to buy Tupi oil for eleven dollars a barrel. The fact is it took us just about 150 years to use up what took over 300 million years to form—the easily tapped stuff, that is. There are huge amounts of "unconventional oil" out there, such as the tar sands in Canada or Ecuador, or the crude that lies deep under the Gulf of Mexico, but it won't be easy, quick, or cheap to extract and refine it.

Peak oil isn't about "running out." Problems begin not when

the last drop is pumped, but as soon as production starts to decline and can no longer meet demand. From that day on, competition for scarce resources grows.

In these politically polarized times, many people are quick to reject information they don't want to believe. So some say talk about peak oil is a left-wing conspiracy to force people to drive smaller cars, or a conspiracy by the military-industrial complex to justify invading a Middle Eastern country, or a Wall Street conspiracy to boost corporate profits. The truth of the matter is that peak oil is merely a geological inevitability that will happen whether there's a Republican or a Democrat in the White House, or whether you believe it or not.

What does all this have to do with motorcycles? After all, this is a feel-good book about riding motorcycles, right? Well, since two-thirds of the oil used in the United States is consumed for transportation, that sector, which includes motorcycles, will be the first and most significantly affected. I can't predict whether that change will be for the better or for the worse. We face a wide range of possibilities, bracketed by the two very different worlds reflected in the imaginary news articles at the beginning of this chapter.

There are reasons to hope for the more positive scenario. Much of the cutting edge work on all-electric vehicles is done with motorcycles. With their smaller size and lighter weight, they're a naturally efficient testbed for developing new technologies. And while electric vehicles don't solve all our problems, they do make it possible to meet at least some personal transportation needs without relying solely on petroleum.

There are other positives, too. The motorcycle industry is more agile than the automotive industry, which was disrupted by $150 per barrel oil in 2008 and then devastated by the subsequent recession. When gasoline prices in the United States rose to four dollars a gallon in 2008, sales of fuel-efficient scooters increased. Unfortunately, many of those scooters got parked once prices fell and people returned to old habits. After a certain number of spikes, or a sustained plateau in gasoline prices, those habits may have to change for good. This could represent a future opportunity for the motorcycle manufacturers. Unlike the car companies, they already have plenty of fuel-efficient models in production—they've been selling them for years in other countries. They've also become the world's foremost experts at extracting the maximum possible amount of power out of small-displacement, mass-production engines. Motorcycles could be seen as smart, efficient transportation, or they could be seen as gas-wasting, non-essential recreational toys used by a minority and therefore easily restricted or banned by politicians. If you commute to work on your dual-sport bike with an Aerostich license plate bracket saying 70 MPG, ONE LESS CAR, you're probably contributing to the positive perception. Doing burnouts outside the bar on Saturday night on a Hayabusa with a MY TOY license plate, makes us look like part of the problem.

To someone reading this book ten years from now, this chapter may be the only part that isn't viewed as a quaint relic of a simpler past, a time when we rode motorcycles for fun with a naive confidence in an unending supply of cheap fuel to drive us. Whether they're powered by gasoline, electricity, or something else, I'm optimistic enough to believe we can continue to have fun on motorcycles that are faster and more exhilarating than cars and still contribute to the solution, not the problem. We can help influence public perceptions, so that motorcycles are seen as a sensible way to stretch out what oil is left, rather than noisy relics of a more primitive era that should be killed off as quickly as possible.

The future ride won't resemble the ride so far, but that doesn't mean it can't be a good one.

INDEX

ABOUT THE AUTHOR

Lance Oliver took his first motorcycle rides on a humble Honda 50 step-through (see "The Most Important Motorcycle Ever Built") and has since ridden just about anything he has been able to get his hands on, whether fast ("Dream Riding in Boomtown") or slow ("Slow Way Around"), old ("Blind Date in Vermont") or new ("Dropping the Ducati"), from the familiar hills of his original West Virginia home ("Almost Heaven for Riding") to the mountains of his adopted second home of Puerto Rico ("Evolution Island").

Over the years, he has worked as a newspaper reporter and editor in New York, Florida and Puerto Rico; as a volunteer English teacher in rural Costa Rica; and as a magazine and website editor at the American Motorcyclist Association. He currently lives in the woodsy hills of Ohio with his wife, Ivonne, and a collection of formerly homeless animals, and works as a freelance writer and translator.